A Mother's Tears

MARCELLA PITTS

PAGE PUBLISHING, INC.
Conneaut Lake, PA

First originally published by Page Publishing 2021

ISBN 978-1-6624-2495-3 (pbk)
ISBN 978-1-6624-2496-0 (digital)

Printed in the United States of America

I heard our names over the loudspeaker, Grace Dill, Colleen Dill, Gina Miller, Marcella Pitts, and a few other girls. A sinking feeling gripped my stomach. It was like being called into the principal's office. I knew some form of punishment was coming. At the least with the principal, the most you expected was detention. This felt much worse. This was different. This was not school. This was my adult life. This would affect me the rest of my life—the one place I never expected to end up. How could it have come this far? I kept asking myself over and over. How? And why? I had no answer.

The cling of the chains echoed in the holding cell—every slight movement leading to a cascade of sound. There were icy cold chains around our ankles. I was trapped like an animal. Was this why coyotes chewed their own legs off? My hands were bound to the chains around my waist, barely able to make gestures. I felt subhuman, like a wild animal on a leash. I could see its reflection in his eyes or the officers as they herded us out and on to the bus. We were seated at the back of the bus, away from the general population. We were in protective custody. We were to do time for a crime that was never committed. Some of the women on the bus were headed back to a world they have created for themselves, laughing with excitement on their way to see an old friend they have left behind. We did not say much to each other, but the thoughts were all over our faces.

The chains rattled as my hand quivered, and my eyes began to burn. My mother's face was tight and stiff in a way that just does not look natural for her. I could see the faint tremble in her lips and the faint shine in her eyes. I was thinking to myself, *My poor mom, how did she get wrapped up in this mess?* I felt like they came after Mom to get me. Colleen was less stolid. A little sniffle came from her down case face. She was always the tough one of the families, not one to show too many emotions, a little rough around the edges. Gina—I could see the pain on her face. She just had to leave her brand-new baby girl. "Be brave," I told myself. And so, I was on the outside anyway. Fingers clenched to fists, spine straight. I pulled up from deep within myself to find the strength I needed to toss a smile over to my family. I wanted them to know everything will be all right. But will it? Will it be all right?

This was a three-hour bus ride. I had sat here on this bus and rehashed the last couple of years of my life. Even though I had lived every minute of this nightmare, I still couldn't believe it has come this far. How did this happen? It had finally hit me. This was not a dream. No one was going to wake me up and say you had a nightmare. It felt like death. My life was running through my head. Was my life over? My babies—how will they make it without their momma? How will I make it without my babies? We should not be on this bus headed to a world and life so unknown to us.

The scenery was familiar. So many times, we had driven these hills. This reminded me of the camping trips we went on with our children—our kids running around, exploring everything in sight, running back to show us every little find. We cooked on a campfire where the food never tasted better. Will I ever do this again? My attention was drawn to a passing car all packed up to go on a trip. Where are they going? Maybe going camping, so incredibly happy, carefree smiling, laughing, loving their lives. The children sitting in the back seat looked up and saw that I was watching them. They smiled and waved at me. For a short moment, I replaced their little faces with the faces of my own children—waving one last time to say goodbye to me. They did not know I was on a prison bus, and I was dressed up in an orange jumpsuit, heading to prison to spend 373 years for a crime I never committed.

My Life Story

Allow me to introduce myself. My friends called me Tootie. My given name was Marcella. I was born in beautiful Ventura, California, on July 30, 1955. I had three wonderful sisters and two brothers. My oldest sister was Princella. Then there was Clovette. I was the next born. Then there was Wayne Jr., my dad's only boy. Colleen—she was the baby of the bunch. Rusty, the oldest of us all, was raised in Hawaii by his grandparents. He had come to visit when he was a teenager. Rusty and Princella were from my mom's first marriage. We lived in Ventura only a couple of years after I was born. We moved on to Coalinga, California, this small town where we spent the next eleven years of my life, a town where everyone knows your name and your business as well. Either you knew them, or they were your kinfolk.

My father worked for Union 76 oil company. Mom kept up with us five kids. We had lots of aunts and uncles—which, of course, meant there was an abundance of cousins to play with. We were a large family and remarkably close. After my great-grandmother died, we moved in with our great-grandfather. We called him Whity. Right out the back door stood the most beautiful wiping willow tree I have seen. My father said the first time I saw that tree, I asked him why the tree was crying. From that day forward, that tree became my friend. I played under that beautiful big old tree for years. Whity also had a big-fenced yard out behind his house. We called it the chicken yard. It was full of rabbit pens full of rabbits. The ground was covered in chickens. Also, in that yard was a covered wagon. Whity would set and tell us stories about coming to California in that very wagon all the way from Oklahoma during the dust bowl. My grandmother and grandfather lived right next door. My grandmother's brother, Uncle

Millard, lived right behind her house in an apartment. We were all remarkably close to each other. I loved my childhood. Whity passed, and Grandma and Grandpa moved to the coast. I had spent most of my life trying to get back the closeness I felt with my family as a child.

When I was thirteen, my father got a job in Bakersfield, California, which changed our lives forever. Christmas break, 1969—we packed up our belongings, and off to Bakersfield, we went. I would miss our little town and all the people that molded me into the person I am today. Princella was married and not at home anymore. She did not make this move with us to Bakersfield. We never knew all our neighbors in this big old town. We did somehow adjust to the changes. Clovette was just seventeen months my senior. She was also my best friend, and if I have my family, I will be fine anywhere. The people here were so different. I was so used to knowing everyone I saw. Now I felt like we lived among strangers—no grandparents, no aunts, no uncles, and no cousins to play with. Daddy worked out of town a lot, which left Mom alone to deal with us kids. We had been there in Bakersfield for almost two years. Moving to a bigger town offered new opportunities as well as new challenges—one in which hit like a ton of bricks.

One morning, I was late getting out of bed. When I went into the living room, everyone had a strange look on their face. Mom was not home. This was very unusual for Mom not to be there when I awake. Daddy said that Mom would be right back soon. He also said, "I need to talk to you." I looked over at my siblings, and the look on their faces told me something was very wrong. They all looked so sad. I did not know what is going on, but I knew everyone knows but me. So much was running through my young brain. Was someone sick? Had someone died? He opened the door for me to follow him out. My siblings watched as we walked out the door, looking at Daddy like he has done something wrong. I felt fear come over me as we walked out the front door on to the lawn, still in my pajamas and bare feet. No, I did not want to hear what my father had to say. I wanted to cover my ears or cover his mouth so he could not speak. The look on Daddy's face scared me. Then these words came out of his mouth, "I have fallen in love with other women, and I am moving out." Those words cut me like a knife. I knew exactly who this other woman was. One of my mother's best friend had started hanging around again. I might only be fourteen, but I was not blind. After Daddy moved out, our lives were so different without him there. Daddy and Sharon got married. He moved two hours away.

It seemed everything fell apart after Daddy left. Mom was so full of anger. Of course, she took it out on us kids. Sometimes, I believe she saw Daddy in us kids, which made her angrier. Colleen kept us busy chasing her around town all the time. She was a wild child, running with older guys, drinking, doing drugs. There was no holding her down. Wayne was like me—mellow. He did not cause too many problems. Clovette was ready to get away from home, and at seventeen, she moved in with her boyfriend. She left me just like Daddy did. Mom and I started fussing all the time. I believe most teenage girls do not get along with their mothers. One night, during a heated argument, I broke my poor mothers' heart. I said that I wanted to live with my father. I called Daddy and said to him to come get me. So he did, and off to Fresno, I went. My dog and I packed up and got out of there. No, it was not what I thought it would be. I had never been away from my siblings or my momma. I missed them all very much. Life was hard for Mom and me. Moving away sure did not help. The sting of Daddy moving on for us kids slowly healed. My mom never got over it.

Starting a new school without my siblings was so very strange and scary. This school was a lot bigger and a lot more students. I was in my second year of high school. I did not know a soul. My step-brother Toby was not in high school yet. I never had problems making friends. I still missed my old friends. My best friend in Bakersfield came to see me for a couple of days. When she left, I wanted so bad to go with her. I felt like I was out of place at my dad's house. I did not feel like I was a part of their happy little family. The holidays came, and I went home for Christmas break. I missed my family very much. I could not do Christmas without them. Daddy was nice enough to drive me home for the holidays.

While I was home, the boy next door had a friend over. His name was Johnnie. He was the most handsome man I have ever seen other than my father. I walked over to the fence that stood between the neighbor's house and ours. I stood in the tall grass, trying to think of something to say. Then I remembered that they asked me to go skating with them. So I asked if they were going skating. The neighbor and Johnnie walked up to where I was standing. Johnnie did not have a shirt on. He had hazel eyes and a tanned body with a smile that made me melt. When he said hi, I blushed. I could feel my face turned bright red. It seemed every word out of his mouth made me laugh. I had a big case of the jiggles and a big crush on this boy they called Johnnie. We spent a little time together during Christmas break. Of course, we went skating every Saturday night until Christmas break was over. I told him I would be back when school was out for summer.

When Daddy picked me up, I worked up the nerve to tell Daddy that when school got out for summer, I wanted to move back home with Mom. She needed me at home to help with the other two kids at home. I was not a part of their little family, and I wanted to go home. My stepbrother would insult my mother every chance he got. He would tell me if my father wanted me, he would still live with me. I did not wait for summer. I came home before school was out. I guess I needed my mother more than anyone. Believe me, life is not the same without my siblings. Johnnie gave me one more reason to come home. Daddy did not seem to mind that I wanted to go home. I just did not fit in that little family.

Puppy love

When I got home, Johnnie asked me to be his girl. I believed they called it puppy love. He was working on some apartments right behind our house. I loved watching him work. We spent every minute we could together. He would stay each night until Mom would say, "Johnnie, go home." Then we would stand on the porch, and our good night kiss would last until Mom would call out one more time, "Johnnie, go home." Johnnie made me feel some feeling I have never felt. I could not wait for the night to end, so I would be in Johnnie's arms again. I was still going to school and rushing home each day to see my boyfriend. He had quit school and went to work. He rented one of the apartments he had worked on. He was eighteen now, and I was seventeen. We had been together for almost a year. Johnnie bought me a ring and asked me to marry him. Mom said, "No way, you are too young," that I had to finish school first. I did not want to go to school. I wanted to be Johnnie's wife.

Getting Married

We decided we would change her mind and knew just how to do it. We were in such a hurry to grow up. On February 6, 1973, my cousin drove Johnnie and me to Las Vegas, along with my mom and my sister, Princella. We were married. I turned eighteen in July, and on August 24, 1973, our little Johnnie came into this world. I took to motherhood like a duck takes to water, like a sparrow in the sky, well, like a mother. I loved being a momma and a housewife—cooking, cleaning, taking care of our little baby boy. We waited for the door to swing open and for Johnnie to walk in from a hard day at work. This is just the way I knew our love would grow and last forever. I thought I was the happiest girl in this world. It was only about a year, and we found out we are going to have another baby. We were so excited that our little family is growing. On March 12, 1975, I gave birth to the curliest hair baby boy I have ever seen. We named him Thomas Wayne after his grandfathers—what a bundle of joy. Johnnie worked hard to support his little family.

Then one day, things began to change. Our happy little home was not so happy anymore. Mother said this would happen. We started arguing about every little thing. Johnnie did leave home a couple of times. But he always found his way back home to us. We were not ready to give up on our forever love. Once again, this was not working out for Johnnie and me. We had grown out of our puppy love. On one of the "trying to stay together" episodes, I was surprised to find we are having another baby. Johnnie was gone again. I let him and my family talked me into aborting my baby. I already had two baby boys to take care of. I so regretted it. I felt like the worst person in this world. I could not live with what I had done. I begged the good Lord for forgiveness. I felt I would surely die of a broken heart. I was mad with grief—so very depressed and oh so sorrowful for what I have done. Only one good thing came out of this. Maybe there was a chance for Johnnie and me. He must still have some love for me left. Despite all our problems, he saw what this has done to me. He came home to help me get over my grief. Now our little family was finally together again. We gave our all, trying to make our marriage work. I finally felt exalted.

God had surely forgiven me, for he has given me back my baby. I was pregnant. The life inside me made me feel alive again. It was only short seven months, and our baby came into this world. We gave him a strong name. We named him Bryan. But all was not well. He was born too early, so tiny, weighing 4 pounds, 3 ounces. I was so scared of losing him. His weight dropped to 2 pounds, 3 ounces. For the next thirty-one days, I prayed to God to make my baby Bryan stronger. With each passing day, our little guy did get stronger and stronger. Bryan was a fighter. At 4 pounds, 11 ounces, they let us take our little miracle baby home. He was the light of our lives—even more precious for how close I had come to losing him. For the first few months, I could not let him out of my sight for fear of something that would happen to him. He was so very tiny. The good thing was that he was healthy, just small. When he started walking at one year old, he looked like a three-month-old baby—so exceedingly small and sweet. He never did get very tall. I thought for sure this time was it—that this time was the time we made this marriage work. We finally had our happy ever after. Our little family of five, it was only good for a short time. Then Johnnie was gone once again.

Gone Again

It just was not meant to be. Perhaps Momma was right. We married way too young. We went from being so in love to being people who tolerated each other and finally to people who could not stand to be around each other. We just could not make our marriage work. We had grown apart. All our dream and all the stars I had wished on couldn't hold our love together. So here I was, twenty-three years old with three little boys to raise on my own. I should have listened to my mom. To provide for my children, I got by being a waitress, working here and there until I found what I needed. I finally found a good-paying job, being a bartender. Wages were better, and the tips were good. I made many friends at the Cottage Inn. One girl, Yvonne, she is my best friend to this day. I loved my job at the Cottage Inn. I had my family to help me with the boys while I worked. Life stayed like this for about a year. Johnnie and I would get together from time to time. After all, we did have three children together.

Moving to Arkansas

One evening, when I was at work, my little sister came in to see me. It was not unusual for her to stop by. This time, she came with an even more unusual proposal. She wanted me and the boys to move to Arkansas with her. She said only for a while. Our father was living out there. I missed my dad. I said, "Why not. If I do not like it, I can come home." I wanted my children to know their grandfather and know what a wonderful man he is. I was sure at this point that the breakup between Johnnie and me and this on again and off again relationship was finally permanent this time—time for us both to move on with our lives separately. I approached the boys with this proposal. They saw it as a wonderful adventure and were eager to go. I did not plan on staying long, six months, maybe a year. It would not be fair to keep the boys away for their father. We packed our bags, loaded up our house, and set off for a new adventure. We landed in Siloam Springs, Arkansas. Colleen kept my boys while her husband and I went to work at a chicken farm. This lasted for about six months. This was definitely not the job for me. I found a little bar on the Oklahoma Arkansas line. I fitted right in there like I had been there all my life. It did not take me long to find a boyfriend. Colleen talked about going back to California. I did not believe the boys and I were ready yet.

I found an apartment for me and the boys not far from work. Colleen missed our family in California. So she and her family packed up and headed back to Bakersfield. I now must stand on my own—just my boys and me. I was so alone when she left. I still had Daddy, but he had a whole other life here, and he did not have much time for my boys and me. Daddy did try to make time for us. His work and family kept him busy. The loneliness for my family grew with each passing day. I got sick with pneumonia and was hospitalized. I realized then I needed my family. Having a family was a blessing to me. I had been here just over a year, far longer than I planned on staying. I was homesick for my family. I missed my home. I even missed the California weather. When I had sufficiently recovered, I purchased the four of us tickets on the Greyhound bus, and Oildale, here we come—lock, stock, barrel.

The boys were missing their father. It was time for them to see their daddy. I would never forget that thirty-six-hour ride with three highly active little boys in a Greyhound bus. We made it, and luck was on our side. I rented an apartment right across from Mom and Colleen. They were both there to help me if I needed it. One of the other would watch the boys while I looked for work. I found a job at the Knotty Pine café. I liked working there, and the money was not bad. It was always filled with fun, laughter, and cold beer. Here I could provide for the boys and myself.

Custody of My Boys

One night, I went out with a couple of friends. I ran into one of my and Johnnie's friends. He said, "Tootie, I am so sorry to hear you and Johnnie have to fight custody over the boys." I was shocked and had no idea what he was talking about. This was the first time I have heard anything about custody arrangement. They are my boys, and no one can take them from me. The next day, I called Johnnie and asked him what was going on. He denied everything and said, "I would never take our boys from you." He was pulling the wool over my eyes. He planned to steamroller me. I never saw it coming. The following week, my mother showed up at work with a handful of papers. I had a court hearing that day for a custody dispute over my boys. I had no lawyer. I was not aware I needed one. Off to court, I went, Momma at my side. I was thinking, *This will be simple. They are my children, and as far as I am concerned, that is the bottom line.* Johnnie tried to have my children removed from my home on that day. Thank God the judge did not see any cause to take my boys from me. I was told to get a lawyer and prepare for the battle over my children. This was when I learned the wheels of justice move slow.

My mother helped me pay for a lawyer. The attorney said I had nothing to worry about. That night, I was sitting at home. My baby was asleep down the hall. I thought to myself, *I have been a good mother. There is food in the fridge. I have never been in any kind of trouble. I do not do drugs. I have a good job, a place to live. I take care of my children. They may not have had everything they wanted, but there is food on the table and clothes on their backs and a roof over their heads.* It seemed to me I have been doing a rather good job taking care of my children with no help from their father. I never dreamed of having to fight for my children. I did know one thing—I will fight this until

I win. I am a mother, and I will not allow then to take my children from me. They are mine. I gave birth to them. I tried to be strong. I worked a few extra hours at work to help pay my attorney. I was trying not to think about Johnnie trying to take my boys from me. I had seen too many bad mothers keep their children. So I believed I would win this battle.

One day when I got to work, just another day, I was tired. My brain could not think straight. I had so much on my mind. I noticed that there was this man over in the corner, playing the pinball machine. I had to know who he was. His face was the picture of happiness and concentration as he played. The ringing of the bells and the flashing of the lights—it was overwhelming. My sister Colleen just happened to be there also. I asked her, "Who is that man?" I added, "Do not let me go out with him. I could end up getting married."

Sis replied, "His name is Rick, and he is your boss's oldest son." Then the news she shared next was a heart-stopper. She said, "He is already taken." My smiling heart stopped at that. I did not mean to get his attention. I had no intention of being the other woman. Rick moved up to the bar and ordered a beer. When his hand touched mine, I blushed like a teenager. I felt my face turned beet red. Then we looked at each other. I could see the same feeling the gripped me also got him. This man was my destiny. Was I looking at the man I could fall in love with? Love at first sight—a second time in my life. Surely, I was wrong. Rick started coming in almost every night when I worked. We sat and talked strictly about our lives. We shared our hopes and dreams, our hardships and fears. Each day, we became closer and closer. It felt good having someone to talk too. We tried to just be friends. Was I falling in love, or did I just need someone by my side while I fight for my children? I was fighting these feelings I have for a man that is not free. I was fascinated by him. I couldn't understand how I can be happy and so full of life when I am around him—laugh at his jokes and have a smile on my face. Yet inside me, my heart was breaking for my children. When Rick would go home, I could not bear to think of him with another woman. I had to make myself face it. I was the other woman. How could I let this happen?

Rick was not married to this woman. They had lived together for a couple of years. He had two daughters from his prior marriage—Carol and Lisa. I had met them and Rick's girlfriend on several occasions. They would come in at the restaurant to eat as a family. How could I do this? How could I be just like the woman that took our father from us? Rick was an exceptionally good father. Somehow, I knew the first time I saw Rick that I was in love with him without meaning to and even told myself not to. I had become the other woman. This was an emotional betrayal. I remember when my dad left my mom for the other woman and the way I felt about her. Yet here I was doing the same thing—breaking up a family just as mine has been broken so long ago.

My court dates finally came up. My lawyer once again assured me I have nothing to worry about. She said we are sure to win. I was nervous, but these assurances helped me through it. I felt as if things went rather well in court. Now we waited for the judge to make this ruling. When that time came, I was so excited. This was almost over. I knew the judge would not take my children from me. There was no reason to. When the judge gave his ruling, my world came apart. He gave physical custody to their father. They gave me visiting rights— visiting rights to my own children. How could this be? My worthless attorney patted me on the back and said, "Try again next year. They will probably give them back to you."

My brain was screaming, "No, you cannot do this! They are mine! I gave birth to them!" I never dreamed the judge would give my children to their father. "I am a good mother! They do not have the right to do this to me! This fight is not over! I will get my children back!" As hard as this was on me, it was also hard on my children. Bless their little hearts—they did not understand why they must live with their father. This I did not understand myself. I never allowed myself to consider what life would be without my children.

They Took My Children

The day came that I was to hand my children over to their father. We packed some of their belongings, filling up their backpacks with their favorite things. I was trying to be strong and not fall apart in front of the boys. It was not working. The tears would not stop falling. I sat down with the boys and tried to explain what had happened. They were upset because Momma was. I told them I would not stop fighting till we were together again. They just did not understand why they must live apart from their momma. The time had come. They were outside, waiting for me to turn the boys over to them. Johnnie did not even come to get them. He sent his wife. I knew he knew this was the wrong thing to do. Johnnie knew I am a good mother. His wife never looked me in the eye. She knew this was not right. I walked to the car with them to tell them goodbye. They stood there with their backpacks, and their little eyes filled with tears. I smothered their little faces with tears and kisses. The boy loaded their selves and their belongings into the car. She drove off with my children without a word. I waved at them till they were out of sight. This was the hardest thing I had ever had to do. I couldn't find my breath. I was sobbing so hard as I was going back into my apartment. This was the worst day of my life. I felt like a part of me has just died.

I finally made my way to their room and was on my hands and knees, begging the good Lord to please bring my babies home to me. This had drained the life out of me. I did not even remember the next week or so. I just felt like I was in a daze. My heart would never be the same. I often made my way to their room, holding their belongings close, screaming into their pillows, begging the good Lord to hear my plead for my babies. I told myself I must be strong for my boys. My heart was so full of pain and anger. I needed to get a grip on myself. I knew the boys were in good hands with their father. But I just couldn't live without them. They needed their mother as much as I needed them. The loss of my children drove me to the brink but also brought me back. I will be strong for them. I am a mother, and they have taken my children.

I gave up my big apartment. It was too lonely there without my boys. I had spent many nights in their room, praying for God to bring them home to me where they belong. I would look, smell, and touch anything of theirs just to feel closer to them. It seemed I could hear the pitter-patter from their little feet coming down the hall, always finding that there was no one there. I could hear the other children playing out our door, knocking on my door, wanting my children to come out to play. I would answer the door with tearful eyes to tell the other children, "My boys are no longer live here with me."

I just could not live there any longer. I moved in with a girl-friend for a short while. It did not take long to get me another place. I was determined to get my boys back. I needed a place to bring them home to. I had my visits, but they were never long enough. This was not the way it should be. I should be putting them to bed every night, getting them off to school every morning. There were so many things a mother should do for her children. It seemed my entire world had been ripped to shreds. The normal pace of my life's symphony was now nothing more than the crash and bangs of life's reality. I was drinking way too much, just trying to numb my pain, just waiting for my next visit with my babies.

Seven months had passed since I lost my boys. My relationship with Rick had grown into a full-time relationship. Rick's girlfriend moved out when she found out about us. She did confront me and said that she would win him back. I really did feel bad about hurting another woman. Sometimes, we think with our hearts and not our minds. When our weekend with the boys came, we would go camp-ing or to the lake. I tried to make our weekends special. Rick asked me to move in with him and Carol and Lisa. Of course, I said yes. I was very much in love with Rick. His girls were delightful, and we got along very well. When we had all five kids with us, I was so happy. I would catch myself watching them playing and laughing, babbling about their lives—a life that no longer surrounds their mother. My heart would be in so much pain. Sunday would come around way to fast. The closer it got for them to go home, the faster the clock would tick, making it time to go home to their father, taking my heart with them. Sometimes, I started thinking crazy thing—like hide the boys out, maybe take them to Mom's, or take them and run and run and run and some more run till we know no one, a place no one knows our names, a place to start a new life, a place where no one would take my babies from me.

The clock ticked. Common sense reasserted itself. *This will be okay. I will never give up on my babies*, I thought to myself. Having the girls around helped me keep occupied. I did not have the time to sit around, crying. The girls did not need to see me that way. I tried to stay happy. It was so hard without my babies. This would all be behind us one day. Mom used to say that every problem is temporary.

Because of the relationship I had with the boy's stepmom, I thought it would be a good idea to have a good relationship with the girls' mother. She needed to be a part of their lives, just as I needed to be a part of my boys' lives. No matter how hard I tried, I would never adjust to a life without my babies. They completed me. I would never be whole without them. My mother and siblings did what they could to support me. No one could remove this pain in my heart. I sure learned early in life that it's not always what you make it to be. This is surely not what I planned for my life. The boys and I had several places we would meet up. We called them our stolen moments. There was a church right down the street down from there house. I would go down there once a week to play bingo and see my boys. They would go for a bike ride and meet me down there. They also told me the route they rode their bikes home from school so we could meet up for more stolen moments. It was a crime to keep us apart. I would try to see them on the sneak a couple of times a week. Where there is the will, we would find a way. We loved each other, and our stolen moments were what kept us going. This had become a way of life for the boys and me.

After I put the girls to bed at night, I would cry my heart out. I had been holding it in all day. Rick would come home from work, and in his arms, I would feel comfort. I felt like his love would see me through this. On a few occasions, I would go to pick the boys up, and they would tell me they were going somewhere with their dad and their stepmom. They would say, "Momma, we will come next time." I would drive away and park down the road and cry my heart out. I could not go home to Rick and the girls and let them see me in this shape. I did not think my babies knew just how important their visits are to me. Rick seemed to understand my sorrow. I did not feel I was giving my all to this wonderful little family. I would never be complete without my boys. I had eyes filled with pain and a heart so broken. This little family loved me, and they were going to help me through this.

Rick's parents leased out the Knotty Pine and packed up their belongings and went to retire in the land they loved and called home, Boswell, Oklahoma. It was not too long, and Rick also wanted to move to Oklahoma. He asked me to go with them. As much as I loved Rick and the girls, I just could not go without my babies. I helped them pack up all there belongings. Off they went on a journey to start their new lives without me. What I really wanted to do was go get my boys and go with them. Then I realized if I did something like that, it would get Rick in trouble. It would probably stop me from getting them back when we go to court next time. I stood and watched the truck pull away. There I was all alone again. What was not broken in my heart was now also broken. I must get through this. I had to dig within myself and find the straight to keep going.

Once again, I went to work at Knotty Pine. That was the one place I felt at ease. I had good friends there. I did have my best friend Yvonne to help me through my new heartache. I moved in with Mom till I could get back on my feet. I just did not feel like I belonged anywhere. Rick and I talked on the phone from time to time. I really believed the love we felt for each other was real. But I also knew we might never be together again. Mom gave up her house, so I rented a room from a friend. I worked as much as I could just to pass the time. I would see my boys on my weekends. That seemed like the only time I could hold a smile on my face. I felt like I was existing. I was so full so sadness. I caught my self drinking a lot more. All I had was eight days a month with my boys. Somedays, I just did not want to get out of bed. I did not want to face another day without my children.

The pain inside me ran deep into my soul. I had lost sight of who I was. Rick had called and asked me to come to Oklahoma to be with him and the girls. He said that once we get set, we would come back and fight custody of my boys. My sister was married to Rick's brother, and they had already moved to Oklahoma. I got with my boys and asked them how they felt about me going to Oklahoma with Rick. I told them we would be back to fight custody again. I told them I would never stop fighting for them. I loved Rick, so I thought I would give it a try. My best friend Yvonne packed up and went with us to Oklahoma. She had nothing going on at the time. She thought her daughter and herself could use a change of life. So now I was back with the man I loved so very much.

I loved Oklahoma. It was a nice place to live. If I felt lonely and wished I had my boys with me, I would call and talk to them on the phone. I could not stand being without my babies. I tried so hard to manage my life without them. With each passing day, I would become a little sadder. I could not see any beauty in this world. I could not feel the love I had for Rick nor the love he had for me. My world had turned gray. I had to get back to my children. This was not fair to the ones that loved me. It just was not in me to live my life with my boys. With each passing day, I became more broken. As much as I loved Rick and the girls, I just couldn't stay. I must get back to my children. So I got on that old Greyhound bus and headed back to where I could be with my boys. That was a long, lonely ride. I thought about how life has been so unfair to me. I left my best friend out there. She had a daughter in school, so she stayed for now.

I got my job back at the Knotty Pine. Of course, I got my visits with the boys again. We missed each other so very much. It was good to be home with my babies again. Sometimes, life is just so unfair. I knew I would always love Rick—just his touch made me feel alive. His arms made me feel safe. Now I was thinking, *It is just not meant to be*. Sometimes, I wonder if I would ever get over what might have been between Rick and me. It's every girl dream of—finding the right man and living happily ever after. I had found mine, and life's circumstance would keep us apart. So I learned to live my life without Rick. Happily ever after only happened in the movies. I was taking life one day at a time. The weeks were long, and the days with the boys went fast. I missed Rick and the girls, and I would call them occasionally. But I had come to reality that our worlds are far apart.

The Proposal

I was at work one day, and Rick called and said he needed to talk to me. He said, "I will call you at the pay phone one day next week." I was waiting for his call, anxious to hear what he had to say. All at once, the door slung open, and Rick walked in. He reached over the bar, gave me a very sexy kiss, and said, "Marry me. We will get a lawyer and fight for your boys so we can all be together."

Of course, I said yes. Once again, we talked to the boys. I told them Rick had asked me to marry him. I promised we would fight for them till we won. They said they were pleased with Rick and I getting married. Once again, my eyes were full of tears. But this time, they were happy tears. The boys seemed to understand and were happy about us getting married. November 26, 1983. I finally became Rick's wife. We were married at his mom and dad's house. Rick was an exceptionally good man and a wonderful father. I was proud to be his wife.

I kept in touch with the boys by phone and mail. One day, I called, and their number had been changed. I called my ex-mother-in-law Mary. She gave me the new number. I would call Mary from time to time for an update on my boys. She told me every time she saw them, she gave them two kisses—one from her and one from me. I called them a couple of times. Then the number was changed again. I couldn't imagine what was going on. The Christmas presents were sent back. I once again called Mary, and she said, "I cannot give you the boys' number. They said if I give it to you again, I could no longer see my grandkids." I could not believe the words she was saying. She said, "They are saying some really bad things about you. They are saying you hurt one of your children." I had no idea what she was talking about. I had never hurt one of my children. This was so untrue. I loved my children and had been miserable without them. The next day, I received a restraining order, saying I was not to call or try to see my children. Oh no! This was not going to happen. They were my babies. Rick and I were both working at his aunt's sewing factory and did not make much money. So we sold a calf so we would have the money to go get my boys. Rick and I loaded up Carol and Lisa and one of my nieces and headed to Bakersfield. My niece Christina was going to spend time with her father. Without any fear, we headed to Bakersfield, California. We knew we have never hurt a child in our lives. We had nothing to worry about. I just wanted my children back.

When we first got there, Rick went back to work by driving a truck for one of his old bosses so we would have the money to pay for the lawyer. Our lawyer set up a mediation meeting. I was so excited. I was going to see my boys for the first time in months. June 4, 1985, was the date set to have our mediation hearing. Rick and I and both girls and their mother all went to this meeting. We thought that maybe the mediator would like to talk to them. We signed in and was waiting for our turn. Because there were five of us, we waited in the hallway. My heart was running away from me. I had never been this excited to see anyone in my life. Every time the elevator would open, my heart would jump with excitement. I was waiting for my babies to run into my arms, telling me how much they miss me and love me. Finally, we were approached. But it was not my children nor my ex-husband. We were surrounded by police officers.

They asked, "Are you Rick and Marcella Pitts?" Then they asked us to go with them. As they took us away, they also took our crying girls from their mother. I could hear Carol and Lisa crying as they led them away. I would never forget the look on Linda's face as they led the four of us away from her. I had never in my life been so scared, and never in my life had I been in jail. Carol and Lisa must be scared to death also. We knew something was up, but I would have never dreamed of anything like this happening to us. They asked if we were willing to walk across the street. Of course, we were willing. We had done nothing wrong. We had nothing to hide. You would think we killed someone the way they were surrounding us. I put my trembling hand in Rick's as we started across the street. He looked down into my scared eyes and said, "Honey, do not worry. They will see that they have made a big mistake. We will be home before the sun goes down." This was the first day of six years, five months, and three days of pure hell.

Going to Jail

Once we got over to the jail, the officers put Rick and me in a small little room, bare of everything except a table and a couple of chairs. I recognized it for what it was. It was an interrogation room. I had seen rooms like this on TV shows. I had never dreamed I would be sitting in one. I could feel my body shivering on the inside. I was absolutely convinced something bad was fixing to happen. We were in real trouble here, and we had done nothing wrong. I was trying so hard to be strong and not show the fear I was feeling. Rick could see this and was trying to convince not only me but also himself that everything was going to be all right. He said, "They will see they have made a mistake, and we will be freed soon." He was trying to calm my fears while being terrified himself. I could hear the waver behind his trembling voice. He held my trembling hand. His hand was firm and not trembling as mine were. I knew he was just as scared as I was. I could see the tightness in his jaw. The way his eyes seen just a sliver wider and brighter than usual. I knew the fear was creeping up on him. I was so afraid. I felt as if I could shake apart. His strong hands held mine sturdily, trying to be strong for me. He said, "It is just a misunderstanding. We just have to tell them we have done nothing wrong. They have made a terrible mistake."

They did not let us stay together too very long. An officer came in and took Rick away. The officer was very polite. He said, "Sir, come with me." He told me to sit where I was. I sat there for a few minutes alone. I tried to hold on to that steadiness that Rick had sought to impart upon me. My brain was not taking this in. It was scrambled like an egg. I could not think right. I took one deep breath then another. I felt the shakiness in my breath. I clutched my hand together, trying to control my trembling hand. I found myself praying to God, "Please let this be over. Let this be a mistake. Let me be in Rick's arms again. Let us go home. Our poor children, dear Lord, hold them near you."

I had never been so confused in my life. Why would they come after us and in such a force? It was not like we were hardened criminals ready to fight them off. We had nothing to hide. We were just ordinary hardworking people that came to Bakersfield to fight for my children.

Finally, an officer came in and read me my rights. His young face looked so serious. His voice was firm, and he was not so nice. He did not seem to like me very much. I felt as if he hated me and was totally disgusted with my mere presence. The hate in his eyes scared me. I felt as if I was really in danger. I felt the room swim around me. It was all my fear laughing at me, telling me whatever worst-case scenario I had come up with was not near as bad as reality. Here I heard detail after detail of the wrong and vile things they say we have done to my children—things I could never think about, much less do! He started asking me questions about things I knew nothing about, asking the same questions with different wording, trying to catch me in a lie. His voice was raised. The things he was saying were chilling me to the bone. He was telling me that we had been molesting my children. I told them they had things wrong. Nothing like this had ever happened. It seemed to me this man did not want to hear the truth. I told him several times that they had made a big mistake. "No! No! Nothing like this has ever happened," I kept saying to him over and over. "You have made a terrible mistake. This is a lie. Who said these lies about us? We never had and would never do this to a child. What you have is wrong." He asked me why I was having sex with children. Why have we run off and moved to Oklahoma? Over and over, I told him that these things never happened.

He said, "We know you did this." He kept accusing me of this horrible crime. I wanted to cry. These were my babies he was talking about, the ones I gave birth to. We did not do this to our children, nor would I ever allow this to take place. He just would not listen to me. He had me like a fish on a hook, just watching me squirm. My thoughts ran off in all directions faster than I could keep up. How had this happened? How could they even think we did this?

Just a bare few hours ago, we were across the street ready to see my boys and fight for them. Remembering this morning, I was so full of joy. I could not wait for my boys to run to me with open arms. I needed so badly to see my babies. I never dreamed we would end up in jail. Here we were locked up like wild animals. This was so wrong. I loved my boys. I would never allow them to be hurt. I stared in the eyes of that officer and said one more time that we had nothing to hide. My words absolutely had no meaning. He wanted me to through my husband under the bus. I told him nothing like this ever happened. He kept saying, "We know you did this. You should just confess."

"Just confess to what? We have done no harm to any child," I replied. The look on this officer's face was so full of hate and disgust. He was already confident of our guilt—had us convicted of this heinous crime before they even met us. They would never find any evidence. This never happened! As I stared at this officer, his words were blurred at this point. It did not matter what he said. It was just a repetition of what he had already said. The words "I know you did this" just kept coming up. He said it was time for me to confess. I told him, "These are my children you are talking about. I would never hurt them or allow them to be hurt in any way. We are just ordinary people. We have done nothing to bring out this kind of force. We do not even have any kind of criminal record—maybe ran a stop sign or two, never got caught." I kept telling him they were making a big mistake. We would never hurt our children.

I remembered Milton Younger, the attorney we hired to fight for the boys, told us not to talk to anyone without him there. Maybe he knew something like this would happen. In this officer's eyes, we were guilty, already convicted of this heinous crime. So now I knew they did not care to hear the truth, so I had no more to say to this man. A female officer came in to get me. They booked us both in for thirty-two counts of child molestation. I just couldn't believe what was happening to us. Who told them these things? My mind was going a hundred miles an hour. I did not know what was going on here. I had never heard of this kind of stuff. The truth was I not only have not heard of anything like this but also I have never and will never participate in anything like this. The crimes they were saying we had committed were all against our children. They had made an awful mistake. We were hardworking people that love our children. I would want to believe no one would ever do this to a child. I did not see how they think we could do these things to our own babies. I had heard whispers of children being molested. I had never heard of it happening in my family.

The officer took me to the fourth floor. She never looked me in the face. I was not sure what she was thinking. Did she have sympathy for me, or had she also find me guilty? With very few words, this officer did her job. I felt like I was being treated less than human, like at the dog pound. You make it in this place—you go into a cage. No one wanted to hear my side of this story. I tried to tell her this stuff did not happen. No sympathy, no acknowledgment that I was not guilty of this awful crime or that I was a human being, and I was scared to death. There she took my clothing, my jewelry, and my shoes—the clothes I had picked out to see my boys and the mediator. I wanted to look nice for my babies. I was standing there without a stitch of clothing on. I felt humiliated. Never in my life had I ever been through anything like this. She handed me jail clothing, a blue wrap-around dress that smelt unclean and a pair of men's boxers, and a pair of rubber shoes—no clean, fresh smell. Not even a hundred washes could wash away this smell. My shoulders slumped, and my defiance faded. I felt like a ragamuffin—nothing fit. Even my hair clip had to go in the bag she put my name on. I felt like a criminal. I am sure I looked like a criminal as well. At this point in my life, I had lost control of anything I do in my life.

The officer led me in a room and said, "You can make your phones call in here." The metal door clinked loudly. It shut behind me. The cling of these doors shutting was chilling to the bone. Who do I call for a lawyer? My husband's with me. Momma—this is what a child does when in trouble. I couldn't call her. This would scare her to death. So I called Colleen, my little sister, my best friend, my biggest defender. I so needed to hear a friendly voice. I knew her well, and she would get this fixed. She had always come to my defense. I could hear Linda, Carol and Lisa's mom, in the background, terribly upset. She was telling Colleen what she knew about what happened. I could hear the panic in her voice. I heard her say, "They have my girls."

Sis said, "Call me back in a few. Let me see what is going on." I sat there on the floor for a while, then I paced up and down this small cell, waiting to call her back. I sure did not feel like a grown woman at this point. I felt like a scared little girl. When I called Sis back, she said, "This is true, Tootie, thirty-two counts of child molestation." Sis would fix this. I had never seen her back down from any fight. I just did not understand what was happening here.

Then the officer said, "Phone time is over."

Sis said, "I will see what I can do to get you guys out of jail." She added, "Do not worry. I will get to the bottom of this." I knew she would never stop till I am out of here.

When I walked out of the phone room, she handed me a thin mattress and said, "Stand in front of cell 44." The door opened, and she said, "Step in." It was like taking a step into hell. The loud clang of the metal door slammed. It shut behind me again and sent chills up my spine. That is one sound I would never forget. I looked around and noticed I was not alone. Nothing had ever made me feel this way. I wanted to run. But there was a locked door behind me. I was trapped like a wild animal—no place to run. I clung to the bundle I had in my arms, a blanket and a thin mattress. All eyes were on me.

After a few glances, they seemed to appoint this lady to deal with me. She looked up at me and said, "That is your bed up there." Then she took my mattress out of my hand and threw it up there. I wanted to yell out, "No, that is not my bed. My bed is in Oklahoma, where I wish I am right now." I felt so timid. I was so shaken up. I did not know what to do or say. Everyone seemed to be looking my way. I felt as if I was a house cat just thrown to a den of lions. As I glanced around, no one or anything looked familiar to me. I climbed up on the bunk where she threw my mattress on. I curled up in a fetal position and tried to just disappear. I needed to wake up from this nightmare. I became one with the wall. All the pain and fears and frustration came out in a sobbing cry that was making it hard for me to catch my breath. I thought if I just lay there for a while, I would wake up from this nightmare. I just couldn't hold myself together. I felt like I was going crazy. I just did not know what to think. I did know this never happened.

I was not sure how long I lay there, maybe an hour. My mind and body were exhausted. I felt numb with my thoughts and feelings. I knew I must get a grip here and figure out what was going on. I heard the cling of the door as it slowly opened with a bang. Then I heard the same officer say in the distance, "Step in." By this time, I had cried myself out. The tears had stopped rolling down my face. My heart was in deep pain, and the fear was so real. I lay there horrified, not wanting to open my eyes to see this nightmare was real. I heard the door clang shut. Curiously, I rolled over and opened my eyes to see my sister Colleen walked in this cell with her blanket and mattress. I got off that bunk, and in her arms, I went. I was never so happy to see anyone in my life. Once again, all eyes were on us. My first thought was she whipped someone over this. I could not figure out in my mind why she was here. Colleen was my younger sister. She had always stood up for me. This was no visit. If she came to get me, why did she have a mattress with her?

I finally asked her, "Why are you here?"

She said, "I was arrested for the same thing as Rick and you."

Now I knew this was crazy. Sis had not even been around the boys for the last couple of years. I knew this did not happen. She said, "They cannot keep us here."

I told her I had been trying to tell everyone that has talked to me that this had not ever happened. No one wanted to hear the truth. I no longer felt so intimidated, not with my sis by my side. I was the middle child and had not had to go through too much by myself. We started talking to a few other girls in there, and they claimed they were also innocent, and some of them had already been convicted. Most of them were here with charges of child molesting. I just couldn't believe all these women have molested their children. I had never heard of this kind of stuff happening.

It was about 11:30 that night. An officer came to our cell to get Colleen and me to take us down to booking for mug shots and fingerprints. Rick was sitting down there in a holding cell. He had been there all day. He looked so tired and stressed out. Rick had worked all night the night before. He had not got any sleep. He said he called his mom and dad in Oklahoma. They were going to see what the heck was going on here. They were going to check on bailing us out. Would you know it, our bail was way too high. We could never come up with that much money. Rick was still saying, "This will be over soon." He was incredibly surprised that Colleen had been arrested. Rick said, "What is she doing here?" He just couldn't understand all this. I prayed he was right. I was all ready to go home. My poor eyes were swollen from all the tears I have cried. My mug shot must really look bad. This was the first time I have ever been fingerprinted or taken a mug shot. With more tears falling down my face, I said good night to my husband as the officer led Colleen and me into the elevator, headed to the fourth floor. My finger still felt sticky from the ink from my fingerprints. I guess now I was on file as a criminal. This must sound terrible, but I was so glad my sister is with me. I had never had to go through anything alone. There were five of us, and I was closer to each of them, more so them to each other. I do believe this would end soon, and the three of us would be headed home.

All we could do now was sat in our cell, waiting for news or waiting for something else to happen. I could hardly watch the news. They had shown us to be awful parents, our faces on the front page of the newspapers, saying we have molested our children. This was being posted all over the news. The press had made us look like the worst scum that walked this earth, saying we hung our children on nails, had sex with them, and made them have sex with each other. We were guilty in their eyes. One should not be guilty till proven that way. Our name was on the lips of everyone we know and do not know. This was extremely hard to listen to. I just couldn't believe we were caught up in this nightmare. I felt as if something has taken over my mind. I couldn't think right. I felt like I am going crazy. My heart was broken into a million pieces. My sister was the only peace I have. I knew it must sound wretched that I was glad she is with me. I do believe once the DA looked at all this, they would drop all charges.

We got to go out to make a phone call every couple of days. We kept in touch with Mom. She did not know what to think or do. One thing she did know was there was no truth to any of this. Our poor mom, she felt so sad that she couldn't help us. Mom did not even know where to start. We cried together and kept her posted on what was happening. One day, when Colleen and I were out on the phone talking to Mom, this girl in the cell next to the phone started talking to us. She said she had the same DA as we did. The DA's name was Andy Gindes. Her name was Brenda Kniffen. There were four of them in their case. They had been convicted of several counts of child molesting. She said they were innocent and had just been found guilty. The DA we had been appointed was not an exceptionally good man. He was full of lies and deceit. Mom said, "Do not talk to her. They are guilty, and you guys are not." It was as if she thought we could be tainted by association. Believe me, she had eaten those words many times. Talking to Brenda put even more fear in me. I have always had the belief that innocent people do not go to prison. Brenda said she just did not know how they got her kids to lie about these awful things. They had been sentenced to hundreds of years in prison. Her family was doing everything they could do to prove this has never taken place. Her family, like ours, believed they were innocent. They said they would fight with all they have till they get them home again.

This was getting crazier with each passing day. Brenda sure did not look like a person that would hurt a child. The day we got in town, the newspaper was lying on Mom's table. The headline was Brenda, her husband, and another couple have all been convicted. I picked up the paper and read the headline. I put the paper back on the table and said, "They did not need a trial. They needed to be hanged." Is this going to be my future? Are people going to tell their loved ones not to talk to me that I am a bad person? I believe most of the people in this world already has us convicted of this awful crime.

Our names were finally on the court dockets—no nice clothes to wear to court. The tier tender did bring us a clean dress to wear to court. I am sure these blue dresses made us look like criminals. We were not being treated well. I couldn't even get a comb to comb our hair. I am sure they wanted us to look like the criminals they proclaimed we were. When we started the trial. If it goes that far, we would have our family bring us nice clothes for trial. Now maybe, we would see what was going on here. I knew I was fixing to see Rick. I loved this man so very much. It would be hard to see him and not touch him. They handcuffed us and put shackles on our feet. I felt like a wild animal—collard and bound. We had to take small steps so the shackles would not cut our ankles. We would not be able to walk into that courtroom with our heads held high. We must shuffle in like a chain gang. We were a shuffling mass of that is weighted down and constrained. The only upside of this day was they put us in a holding cell, and Rick was in the cell right next to us. We sat where we could reach our hands. Just his touch made me feel better. Even together, we just did not know how or why this has happened. Hopefully, today, when we went into the courtroom, they would say they have made a big mistake, and this would all be over. We were to have an attorney appointed to us to represent us in our criminal case. He said, "Do not accept an attorney." His parents were trying to get a lawyer out of Kern County. They seemed to have a conspiracy going on around here. It all seemed a little fishy—not only our case but also the other cases. They had borrowed money from every source they could find. They also put up one of their houses they still owned in Bakersfield.

We found a couple of high-dollar attorneys in Los Angeles, California. It seemed no one wanted to defend us. These two middle-aged attorneys said they would take on Kern County. They seemed to be smart. Right from the start, they did not like the fact that all three of us were standing together. This had never happened, and one of us would die before we lied about each other. I was not sure if they believed us or not. I was not sure if they were even up to take on Kern County. Rick's parents were from the old school. They still believed in the justice system. They said that all we must do is talk to the right person, and this would all be over. They would know the truth, and we would be free to go home. We had talked to everyone that would listen. Not one person around this place wanted to hear the truth. I believed they were all in on a conspiracy to convict innocent people. I just did not understand. Why did they want innocent people go to prison? We had a talk with our lawyers and told them everything we knew about all this. The truth was this never happened. My mind just couldn't put all this together in my head. The lawyers asked, "How did you get involved in this?" The answer was we just did not know.

Going to Primary Hearing

It had been almost a month since our arrest. We were going to court for our primary hearing. Our attorneys were getting us ready for the fight of our lives. Our new lawyers did not have much time to get ready. Not being from Kern County, they did not know how this DA and sheriff's office worked things. The lawyers Dad and Mom hired seemed to be big shots from Los Angles, California. When my lawyer came to see me, I tried to explain what had happened. He said, "This is awfully strange that they had arrested people without a cause." I assured him that there would never be any evidence—that this had never happened. He told me that my oldest son Johnnie would be testifying. The date was set, and we did not have much time to pre-pare. He told me to get myself ready to hear my son Johnnie say this is all true. I told him, "I believe when my son sees me, he will tell the truth." My lawyer showed me my son's statements. My eyes were full of tears, and my heart was so much in pain. Where did my son learn these things? I knew it was not us who told them about this crap. Someone did—one sick person. I still believed he would tell the truth when he sees me.

We had been here a month, and finally, it was time to get this over with. We were all working, along with our attorneys, trying to prove our innocence. We were spending hours at a time talking to our lawyers. I told him the stories of our secret meeting. Why would my boys want to see me if I hurt them? We would go over time line when we were in California and when we were in Oklahoma. Now it was time to go to court—first motion after motion. Now it was time for them to prove we are guilty. Then we got the chance to prove our innocence. If the judge believes we are guilty, then we go to trial. When we got back to our cell one day after court, one of the tier tenders told us that our mother and Colleen's best friend, Gina Miller, had just been arrested. Mom was fifty-one years old and had never hurt a child in her life. Mom's health was not good. She had COPD. Gina had three children at home and one on the way. She was about seven months along. Her children were not even questioned. Thank God they were placed with a family. Two days later, my brother Wayne Dill was arrested. They did not arrest his wife or mess with his children. Wayne Forsythe, Colleen's ex-husband, was arrested. They did not want to let us see Mom and Gina. The DA's office told them to keep us apart. Poor Mom, I knew she was scared to death.

It was time for my oldest son Johnnie to testify. I was so excited to see my firstborn son. He sat up there in that big witness chair, dwarfed by everything around him, and lied. There were no words to explain how I felt when we had to sit there and listen to my boy. My firstborn child was saying all those vile things that the news and newspapers were saying was true. My heart was breaking. I could not believe my own son was saying these vile things about my mother and me and my family. I tried to tell myself he was simply scared. He sounded like he had rehearsed the things he was saying. Anytime now, he would look for me and come running to the safety of my arms, or he would tell the court this never happened. It was wishful thinking. He never backed down, sat up there on that stand, and told the world all this sick stuff happened. How did they get him to lie? I knew these things never happened. Johnnie Jr. got on that stand and never looked at me. He got up there on that stand, describing sex acts between children and adults. How on God's green earth did they get my son to say these things? He kept his eyes on the damned prosecutor. I knew my children loved me. That was a given fact. I loved them so very much.

At that time, I just closed my ears. I could not bear to listen to him anymore. I sat by Rick, clinching his hand tightly. The words that came out of my son's mouth, I never dreamed I would have to sit in a courtroom and listen to one lie after another about our family. He was talking about things I had never heard of. As embarrassing as it was, I had to ask our lawyers what some of this vile stuff mean. He was better informed than his mother. Where on God's green earth did he learn this stuff? He named almost everyone we knew. I would never hurt a child, nor would I let anyone else. As the testimony lengthened, so did the charges filed against us. When my son got finished testifying, I was terrified. If only he had looked at me, he might have told the court that these were all lies, all ugly lies. My eleven-year-old son, my firstborn child, sat in the chair that was much too big for him, describing things I have never heard of. The word that came from his little mouth turned my stomach. I would never forgive them for doing this to my children. They stole something deep and vital from him by making him voice these lies. All belief that your parents could protect you was ripped from him by this trial. They would never be the same. This had been the worst five days of my life. Had they gotten to my other children as well? Would I sit here and listen to my other two babies sit up there and tell lies about us like my little Johnnie did? Without looking at me, he pointed at us and said that we were the ones that did this to him and other children. It felt like a dagger in my heart and soul. Every word he spoke was like a twist of that dagger. For the life of me, I couldn't understand what was happening to us. Lies after vile lies tore my world apart.

As the preliminary hearing went on, it had built out of control like a snowball rolling down a hill, gaining a gigantic proportion. More and more charges were being filed on each of us. Now they were trying to say Wayne Forsyth had a second case with different kids and adults. Now they had put one of the children from that case to testify that Wayne F. had been molesting him and other children—just another smear factor. Later, we learned that they threatened this young man by telling him if he did not cooperate, they would send his parents back to Mexico, where they came from. From day to day, we never knew what was going to happen or who would say what next. The things these children were saying was turning my stomach. I would want to believe no one would do this to a child. I had only met Wayne F. a couple of times myself.

We were coming to the end of this hearing. We had said and done everything we could to prove this did not ever happen. They had added so many charges to each of us. One of the attorneys just told us they had warrants for Clovette and Cliff, my sister, and Rick's brother. One of the attorneys told them to take Bo and Brandy and stay out of sight till they found out what was really going on. There was no need to have them all in the hands of Kern County's DA. They had taken them and went on the run. Christina, their oldest, was the niece that was with us when we came out here—so much for her spending time with her dad. Cliff led his family just steps ahead of the FBI, trying to keep his children safe from the evil hands of Kern County's DA's office. Christina was now in the custody of the state of California. Our preliminary hearing was now over. We had over fifty counts on each of us, and yes, we were going to trial. I could not believe what I was hearing. Now I was frightened. Maybe they did send innocent people to prison. Brenda was sent to prison. She said she was innocent. I believed her. As we came to the end of this hearing, I was praying to God that the trial does not end in the same manner this one did.

Our high-dollar attorneys decided they do not want to take on Kern County. They quit us just like that. They took Mom and Dad's money and took their house. They were out of here. So now we all had court-appointed lawyers. Mom and Gina had their own preliminary hearing. Both of them came up with more charges on them than the three of us—also than Wayne, our brother, and Wayne F. Now that we had all had our preliminary hearings, we wanted all three cases consolidated. We were all innocent, and we would fight this together. Our cell was filling up fast. Bakersfield police department and sheriff department were arresting people all over this town. Now they had put Wayne Forsyth's girlfriend Stephine and a couple of ladies in our cell. This was getting crazy. Homes were being broke up all over this town. Some of the children were pointing out social workers, saying they had also been molesting them. I was not so naive that I think everyone is innocent. But something was very wrong here. Grandmother's aunts and uncles' entire family was molesting their children. I just did not believe it happened. I knew for a fact that my children had not been abused in any way—not while they were in my custody. Someone must help us.

Rick was in the cell right under me. We had discovered we could talk through the toilets. I knew this couldn't be extremely healthy. We did have the cleanest toilet on the cell block. Rick kept me informed on what his parents are finding out. We would say good night every night. Rick was so awfully close yet so far away. We had only been married for about six months. We were still newlyweds, just trying to be happy and live a normal life. All of that had changed now. I prayed one day soon, everything changes back to the way it should be. We had all decided to have a food strike. Day after day, the men and women both refused our food trays. We thought we could get outside attention soon. Someone must hear our cries. We were innocent, and no one cared. Finally, an officer came to our cell and said that if we eat, they will bring Mom and Gina and put them in our cell. The guys told us to eat, and they would carry on with the food strike. It worked. It did hit the news, but still, no one cared.

Just like that, the preliminary hearings were over. All seven of us had our preliminary hearings. All seven of us were going to trial. We all got our cases consolidated. We would stand by each other till we prove our innocence. We were going to court a couple of days a week. Our lawyers were filing motions. The DA was filing motions. With seven attorneys, two DAs, and a judge, no one would ever agree on anything. This trial would go on forever. One day, I was called out to the court. The officer told me it was for custody of my boys. I was very scared to leave the cell by myself. This whole thing had me feeling so insecure. The officer put me in the elevator. As soon as I stepped in there, I saw several men. The inmates started calling me baby rapier, saying, "Do to me what you did to those kids." This was so humiliating. I was scared. They were calling me terrible names. Then one of the men stood in the back, stepped up, and said, "One more word to the lady and you deal with me." He was my best friend's Yvonne's brother-in-law. This man knew my family, and he knew not one of us would do these awful things. Now I knew not everyone believed this crap. Johnnie and the judge agreed to put it off till after the criminal case was over. After all, if they convicted me, there would be no custody battle. I still believed we would win.

Things started to look worse. We had told all our friends to stay away. We were afraid they would get drag into the middle of this crap. We did not want anyone else to get arrested. The children had to mention everyone we know. One day after court, one of the trustees told me Rick had got jumped in the elevator. Thank God he was not hurt—just a bumped around a little. Every time we left our cell, we would hear the other inmates calling us "baby rapier," "child molester." I just couldn't believe this had happened to us. I had never imagined anyone calling myself or any one of our family members those names. Every day after court, all the girls in our cell would meet us at the door when we got back from a long day at court. They would hold us while we cry and sometimes cry right along with us. We were each other's support system. Every time someone left our cell, we heard the yells, "Child molester," "Baby rapier." These were the words that attacked my heart—the words that would shame any person. I am sure I had been called a few names before, but nothing compared to what they were calling me now. The time went so slow when we were not going to court. I had been lying up there on my bunk, trying to go over everything going over my whole life. We should not be here. My mind went nowhere. This had never happened. The seven of us had never been in the same house together. I felt like I was going to lose it. I had my children to think of. They were really going to need me now.

With the thought circling in my head, spiraling too deep, I would make myself get up and write Rick. We both looked forward to the letters we wrote every day. His letters always brought a smile to my face. We wrote about our future, the day we walk out of these doors. He would also draw me pictures. I was not much of an artist, but I did like to write poems. I wrote poems of love, poems of freedom, poems of holding things together. We talked about the life we would share once we prove our innocence. We knew our aunt and uncle were making our house rent for us, so we did have a home to go to—a big house on forty acres in Boswell, Oklahoma, where we planned to raise our children.

Rick's parents moved back out here. They came to visit us once a week. They were working hard every day, trying to get someone to listen to them, someone not from Bakersfield. No one around here wanted to hear the truth. Rick's Aunt Ruleene had started up a group called VOCAL (Victims of Child Abuse Legislation). It was a group of family members having been wrongly convicted. I believe there were four or five other states that had started a chapter of their own. Aunt Ruleene put her whole life on hold to help us prove our innocence. Of course, no one would listen to them. We were so lucky to have a good family who would fight till this is won. Johnnie Sr.'s mother came to visit me. She sang me a song and made me cry. She told me she loved me, and she also loved her son Johnnie Sr. She also knew he would go to hell for what he had done to his children and me. She saw me as a daughter. I also had a longtime friend come up to see me. Julie said, "I have to hear you say you did not do this." I told her then there was no need to come up. Any friend of mine knew I am not capable of doing these kinds of things. They did not even have to ask. When Rick's mom and dad came up to see us, Mom called me out, and Dad called Rick out. That way, we could see each other. We couldn't talk, but just seeing him made me feel better.

Rick and I both found peace in reading our Bibles. The Words would comfort us as we both knew the good Lord knows the truth. There were those mornings if I felt angry at God. Why did God let this happen to my family? Our little children, as well as ourselves, did not deserve any of this. Our families were torn apart. I prayed the Lord would hold us up till this nightmare ends.

Trial

Our trial was set to start on December 13, 1984. Of course, the holidays put things off. So now we just sat and waited. They moved Rick out to a lardo, a faculty where they housed most inmates. I prayed he was safe. We had made it through Thanksgiving without nothing to be thankful for. Now they had put our trial off till after Christmas and New Year. Everyone here was very moody. We all missed our families. The holidays made it much harder. There were no children laughing and playing. No one woke us up and said Santa had been here. We did try to put all our pain behind us for the day. We drew a Christmas tree on the wall and decorated it with candy and nuts from the canteen. We bought candy and shampoo, whatever we could buy in the canteen, and we exchanged gifts and told stories about our families. We told stories of Christmases in the past—the gathering of our families, the camping trips we went on, the photos we could only describe, no family albums to share, the drawing on the fridge. We shared stories that made us cry and stories that made us laugh. These stories were all we have of our past—the stories we shared that kept the darkness at bay. We were not surrounded by our children that we love the most. I did have my mom and Colleen, and Gina was like a sister. I loved that I am with them. I just wished we were home, where we belong. Nothing could stop me from missing my husband and our children. I shared the pain of each of these mothers not being with their children at Christmas. With all this pain in my heart, I still believed this was the most meaningful Christmas I have ever had. I shared it with the family that Kern County had brought together.

One night, I sat in the shower room, crying my eyes out, trying to cry softly for me not to wake up anyone else. This night, there was no point in staying strong for everyone. I just let it roll. One of the night shift officers saw me crying and pulled me out of the cell and took me to a holding cell and talked and cried with me all night long. I told her about how I met Rick. We talked about my boys my life before this all came about. She told me she believed we were innocent, and she hoped one day she would see us walk out of this place. The new year came. We had been here over six months, and now it was time to go into that courtroom and fight for our lives and our freedom.

Our trial date was coming up, and our lawyers were visiting us on a daily basis. They wanted us to remember everything about our life. My mind was still in shock. I did remember my life, the happy life while my boys and I were together, hurrying home from work just to see my babies. That was the life I remember. We were simple people that have a simple life. I had not been able to think straight since this all began. Explaining our simple lives was not what they wanted to hear. Could they not see this whole thing as a fibrous story by our so-called justice system? We worked to take care of our children. We went fishing or camping every other weekend when the boys come over. Rick and I had only been together a little over a year. He asked question after question. My mind was so scattered. I was starting to question my own time line and memory. Somedays, I felt as if I was going mad. I held my truth close and breathed life into it despite the doubts. I had never hurt one of my children. I had never molested a child. This trial was a sham. They were lying. This was just one big lie. We must fight for our lives—the right to live our lives free of all these lies.

It took almost a month to pick a jury. On January 14, 1985, the jury was sworn in—motion after motion, argument after argument. It was near the end of February when our trial finally got on its way. Five days a week, we dressed up like humans and chained up like animals and headed to court. There were seven lawyers, two DAs, and the seven of us. I could already tell this is going to be a long trial. No one agreed on anything. Our lawyers disagreed with the DA over everything. I did not understand what had happened to us. How could we defend ourselves if we have never wronged anyone?

Our lawyers asked if we would be willing to take a lie detector test. Yes, we were all willing to. We had never molested a child, and we had nothing to hide. We all took, and we all passed our lie detector test. Now the district attorneys would not let us tell the jury. It felt like the entire world was against us. It was noticeably clear that the judge already found us guilty and always took the side of the district attorney, except for our family that had and would stand behind us till this nightmare is over. They were picketing the courthouse. They were fighting for someone to listen to our cries, walking up and down the street, holding signs, fighting for justice for our children and us. We needed someone to listen to us. They had made a terrible mistake here.

Rick's ex-wife Linda finally got the girls back. She had taken the girls to a doctor and found no signs of molestation on either one of the girls. Again, we couldn't share this with our jury. Cliff and Clovette also snuck their children to a doctor, and, of course, there were no signs of sexual abuse. We couldn't tell the jury this either. I really did not understand what was going on here. It sure seemed one-sided, and it was not our side. We were fighting a losing battle here. They finally let Gina out on bail. Her baby was due at any time. I knew there was a reason for this. She showed up every morning to sit there beside us and help fight this battle. She said they were trying to get her to testify that this did indeed happen. She told them she was a Christian and would not be a part of there lies. We had known Gina most of our lives. She would never lie about us. I think her lawyer was on the DA's side, right along with the judge.

Gina gave birth to a healthy baby girl. They told her she could go home and raise her baby or go to prison with the rest of them. She chose not to lie for them. When my lawyer said, "I am here to represent you, not your family." I told him we were all seven in this together. This had never happened. Together, we would prove this. So now we got up and dressed like human beings. Then we got shackled like a wild animal, and we were shuffled into the courtroom to hear this repeatedly how we molested our own children. We did finally find out how this all came about. My youngest son Bryan was caught playing nasty at school. When my other two boys were asked, they both denied anything like this happened. It seemed that all the children, in this case, had denied anything that had happened in the beginning. Next thing, this had grown into my whole family molesting my children. This was not what the children said. This was what the darlings and Bob Fields had told them that had happened to them. I couldn't leave Andy Gindes out. This was not a one-man show here.

Now it was time to hear the testimony of our children. Christina, at first before trial, said no one had touched her improperly. Now she said her mother would bring her to our house. All her cousins were there and people there she did not know. She said we would all meet up in Rick's bedroom—knives, guns, boards on walls. She said this was where we all went for bad things to happen. My ears could not believe what she was saying. She said they were ordered to remove their clothes. She described sex acts between children and adults. I had never heard of this sick stuff. This went on for days. At any time, one of the children forgot what to say. It was break time, so they could feed them in on what they need to say. It was plain to see what was happening here. This was a big mischarge of justice, and it was going to keep happening to us. This trial would go on forever.

Tommie, my curly head baby, I just know he would see me and tell the truth. Someone must have told the children not to look at us. Tommie did look over at me then said we lied and made people up. Of course, it was break time. When he would get back on the stand, he would change the story again. Tommie also told them if they could have their toys back. He did not want to be there. It was so hard to hear this coming out of my child's mouth. My little niece said there were screwdrivers up their butts. That would kill a child.

I couldn't seem to write these words down that came out of my children and niece's mouths. I had loved and cared for these children since the day they were born. Little Amanda loved us so much. Johnnie, my oldest son, testified again. He did not even say the same things as he did in the preliminary. My baby Bryan, it was like he was a different child. Bryan was bubbly and an incredibly happy child. He also told his side of the lies. It was as if they were on the stage in a movie. Amanda, the baby of the family, she freaked out when she saw us sitting there. She ran to the judge. Let me tell you one thing—that broke the heart of everyone in the courtroom. There was not a dry eye in sight. The next day, she said she was not afraid of us. She said, "You said if I said what you want, I could see my mom." One by one, day by day, our children sat up there on that stand and said exactly what they wanted them to say. We watched our babies told vile lie about us, using some words I did not understand myself—except for Carol and Lisa. They never lied about us. Gindes did try hard to make the girls look like liars. He tore their testimony to shreds. They said from the beginning to the end that nothing ever happened at our house or anywhere else. My heart would never get over this. Sometimes, when I watched my children on the stand, I would block the words from my ears. The fact I get to see Rick every day was the only good thing about this. We had doctors testifying. They had doctors testifying. It felt like this thing was never going to end. The seven of us were waiting our turn to get up there on the stand and tell the truth about all this crap.

One would think when they have children, they will be able to protect them—not from Kern County. Our children couldn't possibly live a normal life after this. Their little souls had been damaged. Their little hearts must be broken. There were eight of our children that got up on the stand. All had different stores. I just did not understand this. Gina's lawyer did not want her to testify. Sometimes, I think he was sided with the judge on the DA's side. At one point, he made the statement, "I am not saying this did not happen. I am saying my client was not there." My lawyer could not stop me from getting up there on that stand. I still believed we would go home after this. I knew this never happened. Surely, the jury saw this by now. One by one, we got up on that stand, trying to show the jury that this never happened. This was exhausting to the body and the mind. Every day after court, we went back to our cell with our hearts torn to shreds. Our cell was emptying out. All these women that also swore they were innocent were going to prison for hundreds of years. I had always thought that innocent people do not go to prison. I just, for the life of me, couldn't figure out why they wanted innocent people in prison. Clifford and Norma Pitts were not allowed to come to the courtroom. The DA's office said they would be witnesses. They never did call them. The DA's office brought in some jailhouse rats to say they heard us say things about this happening—junkies that wanted out of jail. You would think they would want junkies in prison, not innocent families.

We took our turns, taking the stand. One by one, they made us look like liars. My poor mom, she did not understand this. No one understood what was going on here. We all tried to prove our innocence. No one wanted to hear the truth. This got harder with each passing day to sit here and watch them turn our words into what they wanted them to be. They never came up with any pictures because there were no pictures to find. There was no proof this had happened because it did not happen. I did not think it was possible for that jury to find us guilty. Closing arguments, Andy Gindes pointed his finger at each of us and said, "Child molester," repeating himself seven times. It felt like a lightning bolt hit my heart each time he said this. Colleen jumped up and called him a liar. The judge said, "Next outburst, I will have your mouth taped, [asshole]." Our lawyers got up there one at a time and laid it all out. There was no history of any sexual abuse. All the pictures they spoke of had never been presented because there were no pictures that ever existed. The examinations on the children showed to be negative. This we could not share with the jury or the news. They told the jury of interviewing our children hundreds of times. They visited them sometimes every day, telling them these things happened.

All the children, in the beginning, said this never happened. They brainwashed our children to believe they have been sexually abused by the ones that loved them the most. The prosecution had a good story, and that was all it was—a story, a story filled with lies, a story filled with horror trying to convict innocent people. Seven long months of this and now our lives were in the hands of these twelve strangers. They were the ones that decided our fate. They called us back to the courtroom a couple of times for the jury to ask questions. I believed our lawyers did a good job, putting our closing argument together. I just did not see us being convicted. Deliberation began on July 22, 1985. Now we sat and waited. All of us were a ball of nerves as we sat in our cell and waited. I told Rick if we could go get a motel room for a couple of days. I still had the hope of going home just anytime now. I woke up every morning, thinking if this is the day we go home, or is this the day we start waiting on our appeal.

Then the big day came. On August 2, 1985 (the verdict was in), the officers shackled us all together. Our feet were shackled to each other. Mom's ankles were bleeding by the time we got to the courtroom. We could hardly walk. I felt the excitement of maybe going home by the time this day is over. I just couldn't see them sending us to prison. With much excitement, we sat in the courtroom, waiting for the jury to come in. I was so extremely nervous. My head was shaking, and my breath was shallow. I squeezed Rick's hand. No words could be found. As the jury walked in, not one of them looked over at us. Because of the fact that Gina was out on bail, they read her verdict first. When the jury foreman stood up to read her verdict, the judge told Gina to stand. The words guilty came out of her mouth. I was screaming in my head, "No, no, no, we are not guilty! How can this be!" I could not believe my ears. This never happened. I looked over at Rick and then my mother, my little sister, and my little brother, and poor Gina. The looks on their faces told me what they were thinking. They were like, "I could not believe what we are hearing." We sat there, all stood there day long, listening to count after count, guilty, guilty, guilty. When he was finished with Gina, next, he said, "Marcella Pitts." I stood. There were not enough words to describe how I felt at that moment. I was terrified, and my legs felt as if they were not going to hold me up any longer. The judge seemed to have joy handing down guilty verdicts. Once again, the judge said, "Guilty of all charges."

All hope of going home was now over. As I looked over at my attorney, there were big tears in his eyes. He said that we had a good chance of an appeal. We would not give up. Right now, his words meant nothing. Was there no justice in this world? I wanted to die. I wanted to scream, "Gina is innocent, and we are all innocent!" How could this happen? My babies, how would they live their lives without me? How could I survive without them? For seven long months, we had tried to prove this never happened. There were guilty people in this courtroom, and it was not one of the seven of us. I felt a rage inside me, building up like a volcano, fixing to explode. What good would it do me? All hope was gone for now. I must find a way to face this head-on. This took weeks for the judge to read our convictions one by one. The judge set our sentencing for August 31, 1985. Not a day we were looking forward to it. We sat in our cell, waiting for the day to come for us to see our fate. Would we finally get a date? This phase of our life was over, and now we must face what is next.

The day for sentencing was finally here. They shackled us up once again. They headed us to the courtroom one last time. The judge sentencing us was one by one. Gina, Mom, and Wayne got 405 years. Rick, Colleen, and I got 373 years, and Wayne F. got 285—a total of 2,619 years. It looked like they set a record for the most years handed down. Our lawyers kept talking about how good of an appeal we have. They also said it could be years before our appeals process is heard. I felt as if I had been swept away in a storm with no safe harbor. Mom had always taught me life is what you make of it, that you alone oversee your destiny and the way your life turns out. She was wrong, wasn't she? I had no control over all this. Now my lawyer said, "It's not what is dealt to you. It's how you handle it."

Going to Prison

The ride from Bakersfield was only three hours, but the time stretched before me. I thought we would never get there. It was the scariest ride I had ever been on. It felt as if I *was being led to the gallows for my own hanging. Our destination was California state prison for women. My life was running through my head. I could almost hear my heartbeat. The whoosh sound in my head and chest was drowning out the other sounds around me. The muffling cried the laughter. There was the whisper of the conversion of others trying to comfort each other. Everyone's words were all running together. All I could think of was my life, the life that had been pulled right out from under me permanently. I should not be here. I should not be feeling this way. What have I done to deserve this? What would happen to my babies? How could they live without their momma?*

I did not want to live my life without my children and my husband. How could I go on knowing I may never see my babies again? No more good night kisses. No more tucking them in bed at night. Would I ever be in Rick's arms again? No more firefly in the moonlight. Is this what my life has come to? My momma, my baby sister Colleen, her best friend Gina, and I were all going to prison to do the rest of our natural lives for the awful crime I had ever heard of. We were shackled and handcuffed like animals headed to a world so unknown to all of us. I had heard a lot about prison from the girls in the county jail. They said it was a world inside a world, a world I have never been a part of or wanted to be a part of, a world we should never have to explore. We had done nothing to put ourselves here in this place—this place with gun towers and bob wire fences, a place where they make their own rules. A person became a predator or prey. I just couldn't believe I had not woken up from this nightmare. This was the day I must face reality. This was not a dream, and I was not going to wake up and be in my own bed at home—no more waking up in Rick's strong arms, no more kids running in the hall. This was reality, and it was time I faced up to it.

The mountains were so beautiful. I loved the trees, so many different colors of green. The good Lord gave us these wonderful things of nature to look at and enjoy throughout the days of my life, and now the ignorance and indifference of man had taken it from me. My life would never be the same. Would I ever see this beauty again? My heart was surely broken. And my soul was crushed. As I looked over at Momma and sis and Gina, I saw the same pain and fear in their faces. I just couldn't understand how or why this had happened to us. I hope by saying this, it does not make me a bad person, but I do not think I would have made it without them. I looked over at Mom, the look on her face I had never seen before. Why did they come after Mom? I sometimes felt this was all my fault. I never dreamed that Johnnie would let this come this far. I closed my eyes tightly and said one more last prayer, "Dear Lord, please wake me up. Help me find a way back to my life, back to my husband and children, back to the life before this nightmare." I opened my eyes and saw the faces of my family sitting across from me. I reached down in my soul and found a smile I tossed over to them. I told them this was not forever. Or was it?

The bus jolted as it pulled into the prison and came to a stop. This turned my thoughts back to reality. I saw barb wire fences and a gun tower. This dreaded ride was finally over. As we pulled up to the prison gates, a guard came and searched the outside of the bus, making sure there were no extra riders. I did not know why anyone would want to sneak into a prison. I could feel my body shaking from the inside. I believe this was the scariest moment of my entire life. As I checked out my surroundings, the large gates were topped with razor wire. In the towers, there were guards with guns. I did not even want to think about what it was like in this place. The bus pulled in the gates and headed to the receiving area. The officers removed all the women on the bus that went to the general population. Then it was our turn. We were seated at the back of the room away from the other women. We sat and watched them run the general population through like a herd of cattle. Most of them were just coming home to the world they knew so very well. We heard the whispers and saw the looks.

If looks could kill, we would all be dead. I cringed when I heard the words they said to us, "Baby rapier, child molester." These words were so hard to listen to. I just wanted to disappear. It was noticeably clear we were not among friends, not the inmates or officers. Everyone seemed to know who we were and what we were here for. I felt like the most hated person in the world, both worlds, the real world and the world behind these walls. I had never been hated before, nor had I ever hurt a child. I was innocent of this awful crime. These words cut me like a knife. Nothing in my life had ever made me feel this way. The name child molester was thrown with such deep penetrating hate aimed right at me. The officers had finished running the general population through. Now there were only the four of us left in this room. I was standing in the doorway, gazing outside at the guard tower and the barb wire fence. I was drowning in fear. I felt numb and empty of everything but fear and pain. Looking around at Mom, Colleen, and Gina, I wondered what was going on in their minds. Did they feel as I do? I still felt so alone in the big old world. I wanted my husband and my children. Would I spend the rest of my life here? Would I ever walk out these doors to freedom?

The fear of not knowing had set in. I refused to believe our lives were over. I was in deep thought when the door opened, and a woman walked in. Her voice brought me back to reality. She looked up at me and smiled then said, "I am doing as much time as you, but I do mine on an instilment plain." I was guessing she was in and out of this place. She acted like she is happy to be here. I saw no fear, no worry. This was home to her. I guess if you spent enough time in this place, it would change you. She was making this place her home. Maybe that is why they keep coming back. Would this be my fate to live the rest of my life behind these walls? Would this become my home? Would this place change me to become like her?

Then I heard them call Gina Miller to come to the back. My heart was pounding. It felt as if it was going to just stop beating at any moment. She was the first of us to get booked in. I thought to myself, *This is where they take my name and dignity and give me a number.*

"Marcella Pitts, step this way," the officer said. As I walked through the door, the first thing I saw was Gina. She was standing their butt ass naked. I heard, "Remove your clothing." About that time, the officer told Gina to bend over and cough. Gina thought she said bend over and hop. So there went Gina hopping like a kangaroo without a stitch of clothes on. Even though this was the worst day of our lives, Gina and I were laughing hysterically. It was so hard that we were crying. The reason for this was girls bring drugs in from there rectum. Welcome to their world. The laughter turned into real tears. To the shower, we went. I tried to scrub my thoughts away. The crap on me now would not wash off. We stepped out of the shower with nothing to cover our bodies with. They finally gave us a towel and our state issue of clothing. Once the four of us were dressed, we started across the yard, all eyes on us once again. We heard the chatter and whispers. My mind was wounded tightly—my life, my choices, my time, my name. Now I was number 22530. We walked into the receiving unit. The door clanged shut behind us. I had never seen inside a prison before. It did not look like somewhere I wanted to be. I took a deep breath, trying to hold myself together. This was where we were to spend the rest of our lives. All I had of a life was what they scheduled for me. My tears had dried, and now the anger had set in. Not that it did me any good. The first time they locked us in our cell, I felt like a broken person. I could not think right. Colleen and I sat on the bed and cried in each other's arms. They made sis my roommate, and Gina and Mom were roommates.

The warden was not sure where to house us. They called this unit the receiving unit. All inmates started here. For now, they had made this our home. Several of the other ladies from Bakersfield, Glinda and Brenda and Donna, had all been house in this unit for a while now. They worked in the laundry. We now must wait to go to orientation to see if we could go to work. A job would help pass the time. In the first round of orientation, we did not get a job. They were not ready for us to go to work. They were worried about how the other inmates would react to us. We seemed to have a lot of freedom. Our rooms were popped open at 8:00 a.m. for breakfast. Mostly, everyone went to work. Hopefully, we would be working soon. Our days were long and lonely. We could come in and out of our rooms most of the day. There was a yard we could go out in. The views were cows and a barb wire fence and gun towers. The air had the smell of cattle. There was a dairy farm right on the other side of the fence. We locked into our rooms at count time. There were three counts a day. Then they released us. They told us when the sun went down. When the horn blew, the prison locked down for the night. It was the same routine day after day.

We saw a lot of girls come through receiving that were from Bakersfield. Some of them had known us most of our lives. They did take up for us from time to time. I heard them say they knew our families and husbands and knew this was not true. Some of them lived this out with us in the county jail. At night, I lay awake and listened to the women talked about us out the windows. So many times, I would lay there and hear someone asked, "Have you seen the child molesters? They live in this unit." I would cover my head and fall asleep. The word innocent had no meaning to me. I was innocent, and I was looking at 373 years.

Sitting around here all day every day was no fun at all. I had way too much time to think. I felt like I was going a bit stir crazy. I needed a job, something to keep my mind busy. I sometimes hung out in the laundry with Brenda and Glinda. It made the time go by faster. We finally got to go back to the committee. The four of us pleaded for a job. The warden said we could give it a try. She still was not sure how the other inmates would react to the four of us. We did not get to pick a job. Like everything else around here, they put you where they wanted you. Sis went to work in the laundry with Brenda and Glinda. Mom, Gina, and I all went to work in the receiving kitchen. My days were not so long, and I did not have time to grieve over my life. Having a job gave me a purpose. We worked eight hours a day, five days a week. They paid me $30 a month. I liked my job. It kept me busy and gave me something to write to Rick about. I was working on becoming the lead cook. They liked giving lifers the lead positions. I did believe 373 years I would say that was life. Rick and I wrote every day. Sometimes we ranted to each other, and sometimes we talked about the life we plan on sharing when this ordeal is over. There was not a lot to write about, a lot of I love you and miss you. It seemed we both had our down moments. We tried to keep each other going from day to day. We would never give up on being together again. This might take a while, but we would go home someday. I would never give up on going home. We did not belong here.

The wheels of justice moved slow. It was not easy to adjust to the life behind these walls. I felt if I just rolled with the flow, time would go faster. If you followed the rules, things were not too bad. I sometimes felt like a robot, programing to the same routine day after day—wake up, brush hair and teeth, go to work, write to my husband. I woke up to the same thing day after day. Time stood still. A day, a week, a year, it never changed. The only thing this place did not control was this broken heart of mine. I did not even care what day or year it was. I just wanted to go home. Our family came to visit, reminding us of the world outside these walls, sometimes interrupting the quiet humdrum of the life behind these walls. We waited to hear from our lawyers. They said this could take years before our appeal is heard. I knew we were innocent, so maybe then we would be set free. I did not always understand what they told us, but I did understand this never happened.

Our lawyers were working hard to get us out of this place. We had finally settled in here in the receiving unit. I finally felt somewhat comfortable. We programed and went to work like everyone else in this unit. Then one day, all hell broke loss. I knew now we were not safe. We should never let down our guard. Gina and I were standing in the hall, reading Bible verses. There was a paint crew over in our unit painting. All at once, Gina and I found we were being surrounded by this paint crew, calling us baby rapiers, fixing to kick our asses. I could see the hatred in their eyes and hear it in their voices. About that time, sis came around the corner and made her way to the middle of this mess. She stepped in right between the girl that was yelling in my face and me. She was standing so close. I could feel her breath on my face as she spoke. Sis stepped in and said, "I do not want no shit, and you are not going to give them any." I was scared that something bad was fixing to happen. Would I even make it out of here alive? My blood was rushing through my veins. My heart was beating as if it was going somewhere. There were eight of them and three of us. I wanted to live to see the day I walk out of this place. Then I heard an alarm go off, and there were cops everywhere, telling the unit to lock down. I did not know where they all came from. This time, I was glad to see them. They locked our unit down and took the paint crew to lock up. That was a jail inside the prison where they kept the troublemakers. Now the four of us were lock in our cells, waiting to go back to the committee.

Being locked down was harsh, being locked in our room twenty-four hours a day. I did not know why they locked Mom down. She was not a part of this. We ate in our rooms and couldn't go back to work. First off, we were in protective custody. Why did they have those girls over in our unit? This was no fault of ours. They told sis that she should have stayed out of it. She had always taken up for Gina and me and said she would continue to regardless of where we are. She made this noticeably clear. She said, "What are you going to do? Give me life?" The paint crew said that Gina and I said we could do this to their kids. That would never come out of one of our mouths. Gina said it could have happened to you and your kids. It really did not matter if they would not be back over here to our unit. We gradually got to go back to work and start programming again. We started up an exercise class and a movie night, just trying to live a normal life in non-normal sedation, anything to keep us going.

Now they were talking about the overcrowding in the receiving unit, and, of course, it was us they were talking about moving. Now to top it off, all inmates in protective were moved into a dorm—no more quiet time, no more privacy. It was so loud. One couldn't find peace. Everyone programmed differently in the day. The ones that worked at night tried to sleep during the day, and the one that worked at day tried to sleep at night. We tried to keep an eye on each other and our belongings. There were stealing and fights going on all the time. After all, most of these girls were criminals. I just could not see any of us acting that way. At one time, there were twenty women in our dorm from Kern County. One day, I was lying in my bunk, reading, and an officer from the yard came in and looked around with her disdainfully eyes and her hand on her hip. She said, "I just wanted to see where they house the child molesters from Bakersfield." It was bad enough putting up with the inmates. We also put up with unprofessional cops. Living and working, we saw so many of these girls go home and come right back. They left here gay and came back pregnant. I guess they chose this life—not me. I could never call this place home.

At this point, I was not sure where home is, but I did know it was not behind these walls. I would never be back once they let me out. I did not do anything to get here this time. The ordeal with the dorm lasted about eight months or so. I was never so glad to get moved again. This time, we got our own unit, the one they built for the Manson girls that now were housed in the general population. Now we shared a unit with the mentally ill. What had they got us into? These girls screamed all night long. They did not take showers or clean their rooms. There was never a dull moment around here. You never knew what you might witness on this unit. Most of them should be in a hospital somewhere, getting help. There was no help here. The only help they received was the help they received from us. Most of us were very caring, and it did not matter where we are. It was our nature to help others. Somehow, we once again adjusted to our new surroundings. We had learned to calm down some of the women. A candy bar would convince them to shower or clean their rooms. They might have locked us up from the world like criminals, but they couldn't change the fact that we loved caring for people— something they couldn't take from us. Never had I been a trouble-maker and not about to start now. Some of the women here had hardened their hearts. They were so full of hate and anger. No visits from loved ones or family have given on them—no mail, no pack-ages, no one to care about them. I couldn't imagine what they had done to make families give up on them. I believe most of the popu-lation here was because of drugs. Crimes of all kinds brought them here. Some would not ever leave. Some would leave and be right back. The women in our unit either had a crime against children or had testified on someone. They called them rats. Speaking of rats, an officer called us to her office told us a rat in our case was moving to our unit, the girl that testified in our trial. We were not to give her any trouble. We did not even know what to say about that. Oh well, in the end, we all have the same judge.

My letters from Rick helped me through my days. We were still writing every day. I missed my husband and children more every day. Rick's mom and dad had brought the girls to me a couple of times. It was so hard to say goodbye with tears running down their little faces. It broke my heart repeatedly. My mom's sister, Aunt Peggy, made sure we had everything we needed and wanted—more of what we wanted. The prison provided us with most of our needs. We could receive a thirty-pound package every three months—candies, cookies, and clothes, almost anything we wanted. She kept us spoiled. She bought us TVs. We were so lucky to have Aunt Peggy and Uncle Stan. We had a large family, and each of them believed in us. Everyone came as often as they could. Sometimes, we must remember they still had a life. Only ours had stopped. One day, Uncle Stan brought us bad news. He was fighting cancer. He and Aunt Peggy spent their last Thanksgiving at the prison with us, eating out of vending machines. They were both wonderful people. We saw a lot more of Aunt Peggy after Uncle Stan passed away. We spent a lot of time crying, eating, and, believe it or not, laughing. She always brought a large bag of change, and we would raid those vending machines like children, eating till we were sick.

When our visits would end, we watched them leave, and reality would set back in. It was time for all laughter to halt, and we were back to our world to lock in for the night. One more day had ended—one day closer to home. Our visits were important to us. Daddy came when he could. Our visits gave us hope. But it seemed with every visit only emphasized that even though our lives were on hold, the rest of the world was moving right along. Birthdays, Christmases, holiday dinners just went on without us. Our babies were growing up without us. As our visitors walked out to the real world, we went back to a world where we did not belong. We were waiting for our next visit to see what is going on outside these walls. There were about thirty-five women in our unit right, twenty from

Bakersfield. We were all programmed to do what we are supposed to do. We had a yard at the back to walk or lie under the sun. Our view of the world outside these walls was a cow dairy. We even had a better view here than in the receiving yard. So whenever we did go out at the back, there was the fresh smell of cows—no fresh air. We would lift weights, take walks, or just lie in the grass. Sometimes, I would lay out on a blanket and close my eyes and imagine myself on the beach or in my backyard with Rick cooking and kids running and playing, only to open my eyes and see the gun tower that set right out our back door. My thoughts were only thoughts of where I wanted to be. Sometimes, I tried to put the outside world in the back of my mind. The more I knew, the more it hurt.

Colleen, Gina, and I were going to school, trying to get our GED. I had taken advantage of everything they had offered us. We took a self-help class. I really enjoyed it. A lot of the girls here needed it more than I do. This class not only helped us with our feelings, but it also helped us deal with other's feelings as well. Most of these women belonged here. Like I have said before, this was a world inside a world. It had its own rules and its own kind of people. Some were in the wrong place, wrong time, and then you had the ones that belonged here.

One lonely summer day, I was sitting at the back, dreaming of the times I would sit outside and watch Rick tend his garden. One of the girls in our unit came up and asked me if I was okay. I shared with her some stories about some of Rick's gardens—the biggest tomatoes and watermelon I had ever seen. Just the thought of fresh vegetables made our mouths water. Her next package, her mother sent me seeds. I asked for permission to grow a little garden at the back of our unit. Permission was granted. The day my first tomato started getting ripe, I scared most of the unit, calling them outside to see my prize. I was immensely proud of my little garden—tomatoes, onions, and watermelons. The first watermelon was the best melon we had ever eaten. Mom, sis, Gina, Brenda, and I sat on the floor in my cell and ate the whole thing. Watermelon juice was all over us and my floor. Moments like these showed me that these women were the glue that holds me together. I loved them each dearly.

When given a chance, I went to church. When it was not available, I found peace in reading my Bible. Rick and I shared our favorite verses. Throughout the years, Rick had gotten mad at God. He was no longer willing to talk or praise the Lord with me. He said if there was a God, he would have never let something like this happen to our children and us. Sometimes, this was hard to handle, knowing we were innocent, and our babies were growing up without us. Most of the time, I just made the best out of a bad situation. My job and things like my garden helped to keep me occupied—my therapy. It was not easy waking up here day after day, month after month, and year after year. As our lives were on a standstill, the rest of the world kept turning. I had met some good people here. I now realized good people commit crimes, and innocent people go to prison. I was trying to stay strong, but I did have my moments. We took turns and pushed each other through this nightmare. When we heard from our lawyers, they were saying that these things take time. It seemed like time is all we do have—one day at a time. Rick was not the only person I wrote to. I still wrote letters to anyone I think might listen to us. I had sent letters to governors. I had even sent a letter to the president. No one replied. No one cared. We also had some newspeople come to talk to us. We were willing to do anything to get someone to investigate our cases. We refused to let these cases fall through the cracks, and we ended up spending the rest of our lives here in this prison.

The family had been saying some of the kids were finally telling the truth, telling the stories how they made them lie. They finally saw the conscience of their actions. We were now receiving letters from our niece Christina and Colleen's oldest daughter Windy. When sis received her first letter from Windy the first time, I had seen her cry in a long time. She had hardened her heart and shut down her feeling. I had always known that our children would come out with the truth. The good news was finally, people were opening their eyes to what had been happening in Kern County. Our families were telling us that the attorney general was finally looking into our cases. We were seeing the light at the end of the tunnel. But still, the wheels of justice turned so terribly slow.

I missed my children so much. Rick and I had been cheated out of the love we have for each other. Rick got to see Carol and Lisa more than I do. His mom and dad only lived about an hour from where Rick is. They tried to see him a couple of times a month. The girls wrote to me often. Their letters were a part of what kept me going. Christina had told her stepmom that she had lied. She said, "I lied about everything." She had met up with some of our lawyers and the district attorney. She was on the front page of the newspaper, telling her story. She was so ashamed. She told the world she had lied and sent her family to prison. Windy had already been telling the truth. But for some reason, the district attorney office was keeping this to themselves. This was just the way Kern County ran things. They did not want the truth to come out. I just did not know why they would want innocent people in prison. They did not even know us or know anything about us. If they had checked us out, they would have known better than this. This was a conspiracy to convict the innocent. Was there no justice in this world? If they got away doing this to us, they could do it to anyone.

One evening, we called Daddy just to check in. He said Christina wanted to come see us. I had waited too long to hear this, and we couldn't wait to see her. I wanted to see them all, our children. Daddy and Chris came up that next week. When she got here, she pleaded with us to forgive her for what she had done to us. We all did our best to let her know we have never put the blame on any of our children. We told her we loved her and the other kids and would not stop fighting till we were all together again. It was not them. It was Kern County's corrupted justice system that did this to us and our children. We had so much to catch up on. Christina was fourteen and a very confused child. Her mom Clovette and Cliff were on the run, trying to protect their other two children from the evil hands of Kern County. Chris felt so alone. She was going to live with our dad for a while. This was good. We would get to see her more. Her father agreed that she needed to see us. Her father told me that he drove by our house one day, and Chris bumped up, telling him that was Aunt Tootie and Uncle Rick's house. She started telling him stories about all the fun she had over at our house. He said he knew that day that this crap never happened. Chris continued to write to us and share her life with the ones she knows love her the most. Through our eyes, if the truth was out, why were we still here? This had put the fight back in me. I was ready to go home to my family, my children, and my wonderful husband. These courts had lingered long enough. I wanted to go home.

The day passed with no news. Then one day, sis and I decided to check in with Daddy. When he answered the phone, I could hear the excitement in his voice. He said, "Toot"—his nickname for me—"sit down if you can." My mind went in several ways. Was something wrong? Then I heard the words I have longed to hear.

"Momma." It was my curly headed, little boy Tommie. He said, "Mom, I am coming to see you." My tear scared Colleen. She thought something bad had happened. I said to her, "No, not this time. These tears running down my face are finally tears of joy." I told Daddy I could not wait too long. I needed to see my boy ASAP. The excitement was overwhelming. When the day finally arrived, the officer called us out to our visit. She walked us over to the building, where we accept visits. I was so nervous. I rushed to the front of the line, and the officer asked what my rush was. My heart smiled when I said, "My son is here to visit." With a questionable glance, she rushed on beside me. I could not get over there fast enough. I stopped by the visiting window and picked in for a glance at my son. To my surprise, my Tommie was looking out the same spot, looking for Momma. Our eyes met, and we both ran the rest of the way. All eyes were on us as we ran across the visiting room to each other's arms. He picked me up and swung me around, like in the movies. My baby boy was taller than Momma. I held him tightly, and guess what? He fit perfectly just like he did thirteen years ago, the day he was born.

We talked without running out of things to say. He told me about his brothers and how their lives have not been good without me. It was as if we had never been apart. This was the proof what the good Lord put together—not even the men and women from Kern County could keep us apart. My boys were no longer babies. Tommie told me about the three of them talking about breaking me out of prison when they got older. From the sound of things, they had not had a good life. He told me he had run away from a group home. He ran into one of his cousins and found out where his grandfather was. He said he knew Grandpa would take him to his mom. I told him he had to do the right thing so we could come home when this was all over. This brought a touch of hope back into our lives—a gleam of hope that maybe, just maybe, it will be all right. Watching my son and father walked out that door caused me much pain but happy and sad at the same time. We just needed to be out so we could get our families back. By the looks of things, it was getting closer and closer to the day we walk free.

We were finally seeing some movement from our lawyers. We must go back to Bakersfield. Our attorneys were filing some writs for our appeal. It would be hard to leave this place and turn around and come right back. The only good thing was I would get to see Rick. I missed my husband so much. To hold his hand and hear his voice would be nice. It had been so long. When we headed to Bakersfield, I must say I enjoyed the beautiful ride. It brought back a lot of good memories. The mountains were so beautiful. I took them in like a cool glass of water. The ride this time was like lighting. Once again, this three-hour ride took me a thousand miles. Maybe we would get some good news while we were in Bakersfield. As we pulled to town, I was checking out every car that passed by, hoping to catch a glance at one of my children. Would I even know them if I did see them in a passing car? It had been over four years now. Here we were back to where it all began. They were not any nicer this time around. We got our papers filed for our appeal. My lawyer said it still might take a few years before we get anything back about our appeal. That was not what I wanted to hear. It was so nice seeing Rick and my little brother. I knew the last few years had been hard on us all. I also knew we were strong. The pain of saying goodbye one more time was harder than I thought. When would we see each other again? Would it be years, months? Would it ever end? Now we sat and waited for them to transport us back to prison. We sat in the county jail for a couple of weeks. Then back we went to start over again. They took our jobs and our rooms. Now we sat and waited for the committee to call us back for orientation. Once we got in, we were not happy that they took our jobs. They said that we could not work around the general population anymore. We had never had any trouble working in the receiving kitchen. I loved my job and my boss. Oh well, time to move on. We were getting a lot of publicity right now. The committee did not want to take a chance on us getting hurt.

Now I had way too much time to think—a visit from my son, got to see my husband—a touch of my life before Kern County tore it apart. Now I was falling into a depression. The gray was moving in, and I did not know what to do. What if we never go home, if I never get to see my son Tommie again or hold my husband's hand? I was beginning to think we would never go home. Are we doomed? I guess my patience had run out. I fullheartedly believe what the love that Rick and I shared was real. I would always love him. I believe now was the time to set him free. Maybe he could find a new love that could come see him. This was not what I wanted. I felt I had no choice. I had always heard if you love something, set it free. If it was yours, it would return. I asked Rick to divorce me. (He did.) I did not know what I was thinking. I guess I was not. I was so filled with guilt. I blamed myself for this because it started with my children. Rick was a wonderful man, had a wonderful life with his two wonderful daughters. When I came into his life, it all changed. I had torn his world apart. I did not want to drag him into my depression.

It seemed everything was falling apart. Mom fell and broke her leg. She had to have surgery on it. They housed her in the prison hospital. We were worried about her the whole time she was gone. Next, sis had been having some problems. When they took her to the hospital, they found cancer. She had ovarian cancer.

They were going to do laser surgery. They got her in fast. When they brought her back to our unit, it was count time, and we were all locked in our rooms for the count. Mom asked the guard if she could go check on her daughter. He said, "You gave up your mother button when you came to prison."

Mom yelled back, "I did not choose to come to prison, you prick!" He wrote her up, and she got fifteen days of lockup. Thank God she got to stay in her own cell. Sis was fine in a couple of weeks, and they got all cancer. On top of being depressed, the holidays were here. We had our Christmas party right outside Moms' room. She was still on lockdown. She did not miss a thing. I was so glad to see another year went by. Hopefully, we would go home this year. At this point, I was ready for more bad news. One day, it came. It came in like a storm. We had received a call from our brother-in-law, Russel. We were told to call him. He told us Princella was extremely sick. This was hard on us not being able to get to our loved ones when we knew they needed us. Princella died that evening. My poor mother, after all we had been through, she lost her firstborn daughter. Princella had four children. We never did find out what killed her at the age of thirty-four. We had talked to her. Mom called her every couple of weeks. The last time I spoke to her, I could tell something was not right. She blamed it on the kids, saying they were wearing her out. She was hiding something from us. Princella never did get to come see us. She did not want to be in prison with the rest of us. Her husband was afraid if they came around, they might be arrested. They had no questions of our innocence. But we were also in prison. They knew we would never hurt a child. When we were in the trial, her husband came to our court to see what was going on. One of my boys was on the stand. When Russell walked into the courtroom, my son stood up, pointed him out, and said, "That is my uncle." He was questioned and let go. That was the last time they came around. I couldn't blame them. They had four children to protect. I always thought she grieved herself to death. I did not know what would happen to her children. The officer that worked that night let sis and I lock in Mom's room with her. I thought that was nice of her. Like all professions, you have good and bad. RIP, Princella, till we meet again.

Here we go. It was time to go to the orientation again. Well, the committee had concluded it was time for me to stand on my own. They were sending me to the general population. They said that I depended on sis and Mom way too much. Yes, I did. It had always been this way. We were family. It was supposed to be like this. No matter where we were, we were family first. The day came when they told me to pack my stuff. I packed my things, trying to hold back my tears. Colleen and Mom were so upset. I said my goodbyes, hugged them all, and with a smile on my face to hide my fears—not wanting Mom and Colleen to see just how frightened I really am. Off I went across the yard to my new unit. I was petrified. I was not incredibly happy about this move. Like I have said before, my life's decisions are no longer my own. As I walked over there, everyone looked our way. My father had tried to put a stop to this move. No luck. Here I went. They roomed me up with a girl that had once lived in the same unit as me. She had lived over there in protective custody for more years than I. A few months ago, they also decided it was time for her to go to the general population. I just hoped this worked out. I got a job in the kitchen. We fed four thousand women three times a day. Daddy got permission to call the three of us out at once—the only way I got to see Mom and Colleen. They were upset about all the weight I had lost. I tried to keep a smile on my face during the visit. I tried not to let them know I lived in constant fear. Food was the last thing on my mind. I hated it over here in this yard all by myself. Every time our door popped open, I jumped like I had been shot. I was doing everything I could to fight this fear that is trying to take me over.

My job was the only enjoyment I got. I had always love to cook. This was when I felt at ease. I had met a couple of girls. I had never had a problem finding friends. Most women here did not see me as a friend. They saw me as a convicted child molester. I missed my momma and sister and all the girls that now see me as family. I only came out of my cell when I went to work. I finally got brave enough to go over to the canteen. I only went twice. The fears inside told me not to go. I still heard the whispers, "There she goes, the child molester." I would just walk along like I did not hear. Every morning, I was awakened with fear. You would think after being locked up all these years, I would have toughened up some and start living like the rest of these women. I couldn't. It was just not in me. I did not belong here. I had not and would not let this place and these people change me. This was the first time I had ever been alone like this—no family to back me up, no safe place to hide, no protective custody over here. I was on my own. I said I was alone. I was wrong. Three weeks before we were arrested, my brother-in-law Cliff and I were baptized. The good Lord would never leave me.

One day while I was at work, one of the girls from the pain crew came through the lunch line. I did not even see her till she spoke. I looked up, and she made the gesture that she was going to cute my throat. I did tell my boss about this. He liked my work and wanted to keep me safe. He came to get me for work. Then he walked me back to my cell every night when my day was over. I tried to get them to send me back over to Mom and Colleen. The officer told me it was just a threat. I was not harmed. Believe me, this was harming both my body and my mind. I couldn't eat or sleep. Every little sound sent me into a panic, always feeling I was in danger, always watching my back. I had never been so along in my life. A couple of weeks went by, and I was starting to feel a lot better. One day while I was at work, in walked four officers. We were all watching them, knowing they had come for someone. They walked right up to me. One of the officers said, "There is a treat out for your life. You must go back to protective custody." I was so glad they were taking this seriously. They escorted me to my cell and watched me pack up my belongings. Off to lock up, I went. This was a new building. The women that were housed here couldn't stay out of trouble. They were the worst of the worst. This was a prison inside a prison. I was not in trouble. I was here for my safety. Nowhere else to put me—so they said. I asked to go back over there where Mom and sis are. Not yet, they said. I must sit here till my name comes up for another visit to our committee. This could take a while.

This building was called gray stone. Believe me, that is what it was made of, cold gray stone. There was no peace here. These girls cussed and screamed at each other. Sometimes, I prayed for peace and quiet. I got to go outside for an hour twice a week. Every other day, I got out for a shower. We even ate in our rooms. There was one small window to look out. This was lonely, and I felt the sadness taking over. This place was dull and regimented as it brought the depth of emotions out of me. I felt I would never have in the outside world. I had never noticed the beauty in the clouds till I was put in this little room, and all I had was a window and my mind to keep me occupied. I would sit on my metal desk and try to drown out the yelling and hateful words they yelled across this cold stone building out at each other. I would sing my heart out to my old country songs about going home—the song I sang as a child—and cry till I could not cry anymore, watching the beautiful clouds go by. No TV or radio—all I have was time. My mind went so many different distractions. I spent too much time sitting in this cell. They let me keep my visits. I was not in trouble. I was in danger.

My dad worked it out, so he could call Mom, Colleen, and I all out to visit at once. That was the only way we could see each other till I moved back over there. They kept me locked in the cell for way too long. When they finally called me into the committee, of course, they were sending me back over to my family, where they should have left me in the first place. It was like a party when I finally returned over to my unit. There were hugs all day long. It was like a homecoming. How could I call this place home? It was such a relief getting back over where I felt safe, and if I was not safe, I had plenty of backup. Mom and all the girls loved and missed me. I promise I did miss them more. It did not take long for things to go back to normal—not normal for long. We were all called together and told we were all moving to gray stone—troublemakers on the top floor and protective custody on the bottom floor. Some of the other girls were being sent to other prisons or sent to the yard—the general population. Not sure when the change would take place.

Our appeal had finally gained some momentum, finally making its way to the appellate court. They said our appeal was finally being heard. Again, they said that things like this just take time. Six long years, we had hoped and hoped a little more. Now my hope had become shallow, and I wondered, *Will we ever be free?* The trip to the yard had left its mark on me that I just couldn't shake. We had all got most of our stuff packed for our move, waiting on the word. Tomorrow was the day. We were off on a new adventure. We were all locked up for the count. My door popped for some reason. I stuck my head out the door, and the officer on duty called me out. This was not normal. No one left their cell during the count. I walked slowly to the front, thinking, *Here comes more bad news.*

When I got to the front, the officer looked at me and smiled, and she handed me a rose and said, "Call your lawyer." I grabbed the rose, and with a trembling hand, I ran to the phone area. With my shaky fingers, I dialed my lawyer's number. While I was dialing the number, the officer started popping the doors to all the girls from Bakersfield. I could hear the excitement in my attorney's voice. He said, "Pack your bags. You are going home." That was all I heard. I had to call him back. We danced. We hugged and cried—happy tears at last. I did not hear another word my attorney said. "You are going home" did it for me. This was December 5, 1990. Once again, he said this could take some time. This did not seem right. If we won our appeal, we wanted to go home. Okay, wait again. I still couldn't believe it. We kept that phone line going, calling our loved ones, ringing in the good news. This was finally over. We were coming home. Finally, we could see the light at the end of the tunnel. They went ahead and moved us to gray stone. Knowing this would not work, we at least got to work. I worked on the yard crew with sis and Gina. This made the time go faster. We stayed there for about two months and waited to go home. There was no news yet. We were still waiting on the paperwork.

Now they called us into the committee again and said, "You are all moving to Sacramento prison." We told them we won our appeal, and we were going home. One of the committee members said, "Jesus is coming tomorrow." And they shipped us off to Stockton. Gina moved to the general population. She did not make the move with us. It was hard to leave her behind. There was no choice. We lost the ability to make our own decisions over six long years ago. Maybe Gina would be fine now that we won our appeal. When we got to Stockton prison, I tried not to settle in. There were no pictures on the walls. I did not even unpack some of the stuff I wanted to take home. With every sunrise, I said a prayer, "Dear Lord Jesus, let this be the day we receive freedom. Then I can settle in somewhere, not here in this prison."

One night right before lock-in, one of the officers on duty came up on sis and me and said, "Take care of your momma." She made it sounds like she was not working at our unit anymore. She said, "Yes, I will be here," and off she went. *Oh my, is she telling us we are going home tomorrow?* I am hoping. Colleen and I were roommates. We could not sleep. We did our hair, ready to go home. I found myself thinking about Rick, wondering if he would want me back. After all, I did ask him for a divorce, hoping we did not misread this officer. We talked most of the night. We were up with the sun, just waiting to hear something. Then all at once, we heard over the loudspeaker, "Grace Dill, Colleen Bennett, and Marcella Pitts, roll up for release." I could not believe it. We were going home on December 5, 1990. Gina was all alone to walk out those gates. I wanted to be at CIW when we were released. So I could turn around and tell them I told you so. They popped the door in our unit so we could say our good-byes. Aunt Peggy sent us new clothes after we won our appeal. The three of us are dressed to kill. I could see the sparkles in Colleen's and Mom's eyes. But I could also see what this had done to them. The van pulled up, and they told us to load our stuff. I hated leaving Brenda. I know she was happy for us. I hope this gave her hope that she would be out right behind us. I loved Brenda like a sister. It was hard leaving her behind.

We loaded up our belongings, and the driver took us to the same office we came in to. They said, "Leave your belongings in the van. I will be taking you to the Greyhound bus station." Once the paperwork was finished, they gave us the money we had on our books. We asked about our gate money. When she said it might take a while, we decided not to wait. If we were free, we were leaving. They could mail it to us or keep it. We did not want to spend one more minute in prison. We were *free*. The driver drove up to the Greyhound bus station, helped us get our belonging, said good luck, and drove off. Just like that, we were free. We just stood there, looking at each other. Then we began to laugh and cry at the same time. When we finally went in, we pulled all our money together and bought three tickets to Bakersfield, California, back to where it all began. This time, no chains were around our ankles and no handcuffs on hands. Now we were free. I loved saying that.

While waiting on our bus to Bakersfield, we went to the phones. Of course, we called Clovette first. We screamed into the phone, "We are free!" We did one call after another. I needed to calm down. I thought a cigarette would help. I walked up to the security cop and asked if I could go outside for a smoke. He responded, "Lady, far be it from to stop you." I looked over at Mom and sis, and they were laughing at me. I was so programmed to ask before to do any little thing. I had almost forgotten my life is mine again. I could go where I want to go. I was free, free to eat, free to do what I want, free to go where I want. I was free on my way home, wherever home may be—no more fences, no more walls. We were no longer guarded with guns. This was the first day of the rest of my life, the end of six years, five months, and one day of pure and utter hell. And now it was all over with. Just like I had told everyone, we would go home—finally, on our way to freedom.

The Last Bus Ride

On December 5, 1990, we were free. We sat at the bus station, waiting to leave on our last bus ride. We were finally going home. It took four hours to get back to Bakersfield, back to where it all began. I had four short hours to figure out which way to go. We would have had someone at the gate to pick us up. But we did not know for sure that today was the day we go home. Yes, finally, we were headed home. Home, I just loved saying that. This was really happening. I hope Rick would have me back. I twisted my wedding ring around on my finger, saying a prayer, then I went back to the day Rick put that same ring on my finger for the first time, the day we planned to spend our lives together. I also thought about my stupid decision to ask for a divorce. I loved him very much. I couldn't wait to get home to him. I had called Rick's mom and dad, and they told me Rick would not get out for a couple more days. We were only married six short months when this all started. I prayed he takes me back. We were so in love with lots of dreams. The last couple of years had really been hard. I was beginning to think we would never go free. I had always wanted to be Rick's wife. I wanted to grow old together. I was just really stressed out. Today, I was among the happiest women alive. I was going home, hoping to be Rick's wife again. I did not know where our house would be or what town we would live in. Going home to me right now was being in my husband's arms and the laughter of our children. That is where I wanted to be. I hoped his plans include me. Asking for a divorce just might have destroyed our relationship.

I was not sure how freedom feels like yet. We were all jumpy. There was not a place on the bus for me to sit by Mom and sis. So I looked around for the nicest face and sat by her. I was hoping she did not ask me a bunch of questions. I just wanted to get to Bakersfield and figure out the rest of my life. She asked me where I was going. I said, "We have been in Stockton and going home to Bakersfield." She could tell I did not want to talk. If she saw the news tonight, she would know where I had been. I never did tell her that I was just released from hell. This just did not feel real. This bus was taking me to freedom, back to the life I started six years, five months, and one day ago. This guy on the bus asked Colleen how long we had been down. I just did not know how he could tell. Was it so obvious? We were all dressed up in the nice new clothes Aunt Peggy sent us—maybe the way we carried ourselves. Would everyone look at us like that? Would they know where we just got released from prison? I wonder what Mom and Colleen were thinking. I know my mind was going so many different directions. I looked back at Colleen and Mom, and the smile on their faces looked a bit questionable. Just like myself, I was happy, but the unknown was scary. The bus was full by the time we got to Bakersfield. I felt like I could get there fast if I got out and ran. I was so full of energy. Over six long years of being locked up like animals, walking back into society might not be the easiest thing I had ever done. One thing I knew for sure was not the hardest. If this did not break me, I was sure nothing would.

When we pulled into the bus station, we could see the press everywhere. Colored lights were going in every direction. We tried to make the press think we were flying into Bakersfield. You just couldn't ditch the press. Our cousin Bobbie was there to pick us up. She had seen on the news that we had been released. There was also one of the women we were in prison with. Glinda was also there. We rushed Mom out of there. Our cousin Bobby smuggled Mom away. We told her we would talk to the press. If we did not talk to them now, they would hound us relentlessly. Colleen and I sat down with the press and tried to answer questions. Where would we live? What about our kids? Their words were hitting the walls of my brain, and the words were coming together. We had no answer at the time. We had no idea what life has in store for us. We were starting over from scratch—not even an ash left of our former lives.

On June 4, 1984, six years, five months, and one day ago, Kern County took everything from us but our lives. I was a nervous wreck.

I couldn't think right now. Our lungs were not full of free air yet. After our brief talk with the press, Colleen and I headed to good old Oildale. We went to Glenda's house and did some calling around. Colleen's oldest daughter Windy was there, and Colleen called one of her friends to come get her. When I saw Colleen and Windy hug, my heart jumped a beat. Would I ever get to hug my boys again? Colleen left, and I wanted to go to Rick's mom and dad's house. I felt sorry for Windy. Her mother did not even ask her to go with her. So I took her with me. I was hoping for a reunion myself. Carol and Lisa might be over at Rick's mom and dad's house. It was only a couple of blocks away. We chose to walk or, in my case, run. I had not been home an hour, and here I was walking down the streets of Oildale with my sixteen-year-old pregnant niece. I was scared to death, not sure exactly what I was afraid of, but I was. We hurried down the road as fast as I could, keeping an eye on everything around me. Windy laughed at me. She said, "Aunt Tootie, no one is after you. It is okay." I was not okay. I felt so strange in this open space, no fences with barb wire, going where I chose to go, walking in and out any door I chose to walk in. Right now, I needed to get to my family—if they still wanted me.

When I walked through the gates of the house of Rick's parents, it finally hit me. I was free. This was home. The front door slammed open, and out came Carol and Lisa screaming and calling my name, running into my arms. There were tears falling down our faces as we embraced, never wanting to let them go. I prayed to God right there and then to never separate us again. Now I was home, holding the ones I loved so very much. The day would come, and my boys would come to me. I would pray for this every day till we are together again. We walked into the house. Rick's parents were sitting there, waiting for me to get home. This was finally feeling real. I was free. We were all talking at once, the laughter, the smiles. My heart was running over with joy. One of the neighbors, Nellie, called out to me and said Rick was on the phone. I ran over there, and Nellie handed me a phone. This phone did not have a cord. With a puzzled look on my face, I asked where do I plug this in. She said, "Just talk. It is cordless."

"Cordless?" I said, "Hello, honey, this phone has no cord." He said a lot had changed while we were away. I was afraid he would say it was over between us. The next words out of his mouth was "I love you, and I cannot wait to hold you." He told me he always loved me, and *yes*, he wanted me to be his wife. Hearing his voice filled me with excitement. I know I loved him more than ever. After Rick's call, I felt better and more at home than ever. I know Rick would be home to help me adjust. We all sat and talked for hours—so many stories to tell. The girls had to go homeschool tomorrow. It was getting late. They needed to go home. They promised they would see me tomorrow after school.

Rick would be home in two days, not two months or two years, just two short days. I would be in the arms of the man I love so very much, and I should never be alone or feel so lonely ever again. We were released by fax. The men's prison won't release them till it comes in the mail. I had enough. I could do this in the next couple of days. Rick's mom and dad said I could stay there with them. But Windy asked me to stay with her. I felt bad that she just got her mother back, but she did not take her with her when she left. Colleen should have taken her. I guess sis needed some time to figure out which way to go in her new life. I went with Windy and spent my first night of freedom, not in a bed, but I slept on the cold, dirty floor. I did not sleep much anyway. I had a lot going on in my mind. My boys, where were they? I did not know if I should go look for them or wait till they come to me. Should I start making calls? We were all over the news. I hoped and prayed they saw me on the news. I longed for the day they run to me like Carol and Lisa did, rushing by my side, never to leave me again. This felt very lonely and out of place. I was feeling a lot of anxiety. My mind was racing, telling me the cops are going to come and get me any time, saying they made a mistake and must take me back. This fear was so real to me. I might never trust again. I thought Colleen would be with me till Rick got home so I would not be alone. We all went in different ways. I did not even know where Gina is. I knew she was out. I would find her when Rick gets home.

The next morning, I got up and went over to Rick's mom and dad's house. I knew Carol and Lisa would be there to visit with me.

Mom fixed us breakfast. I asked if I could help. She turned me down. She smiled and danced around the kitchen as she cooked. The smell of breakfast made me smile. This sure smelled like home to me. I shared my desire to move back to Oklahoma. By the sound of it, they would go back very soon. I couldn't wait to cook breakfast for my family. I would find my way and have my own home soon. We sat and talked most of the day, telling them story after story. I could talk for days. I was so full of happiness. Yet deep inside, I was still filled with fear. Rick would be home tomorrow. Then I would be better. I called my best friend, Yvonne. She did not even know I was home. She said she did not watch the news. We had talked a few times in the last few years. She came over to see me, and we took offs to see some old friends. When she started her car, the seat belt flung over me. I jumped like I was shot. I thought someone was in the back seat and threw something over my head. I must get rid of this fear that is living within me. It was wonderful seeing Yvonne again. It was like we have never been apart. Being free was going to take a while getting used to. I was very jumpy, and the world felt like it is turning in full speed—so fast it made me dizzy. I was not sure what to do with myself. Once Rick was home with me, we could take a minute and take this all in together. Just one more day. Tonight, I lay down to sleep—if I could sleep. This was the last lonely night I would spend without my husband. Then maybe I could get a grip on myself and breathe in the fresh free air once again.

Today, December 7, 1990, was the day Rick, my little brother Wayne, and Wayne Forsythe were all coming home. First off, we must go to the jail and bail Rick out. This is because he was busted in prison with a joint. Rick had to be released from the county jail. My brother and Wayne F. were released from prison. I believe they were in different prisons. Rick was coming in from Tehachapi Prison, about an hour drive from Bakersfield. When we got up to the jailhouse, there was press everywhere. I was standing out in the parking lot, talking to the press when Carol and Lisa got there. They came running across that parking lot, almost knocking me down. We were hugging, crying, and laughing—finally happy tears—waiting for Rick's bus to arrive. "Here he comes!" someone yelled. The girls and

I grabbed hands and ran to see him. The smile on his face was the biggest smile I have ever seen. He was seeing his wife and daughters together again for the first time in six years, five months, and three long days. We ran up the stairs to the jail, standing right outside the door we walked into on June 4, 1984, where they tore our family apart. We were walking in holding hands, now waiting for him to be in my arms once again, waiting on that door to open for the last one of the seven of us to walk into freedom. I heard, "Hit 1." The door popped open, and Rick walked out and into the arms of his children and wife—finally free to be a family again, free to make choices, free to live our lives the way we choose. It seemed we have come full circle where this nightmare started. It now came to an end—six years, five months, and three days ago. Rick said, "It will all be okay." Five of us walked in here together, and now the same five walked out together. Now we were together again, free to start a new life together with the way we choose. It would be okay. We were all together again. I believe my boys would be the next to come home.

We spent most of the day at Rick's mom and dad's house. It was so wonderful to see just how many friends and families we had backing us up. People were coming in and out all day. I checked on Mom and Colleen. They were both just trying to get a grip on all this. They were with friends and family and doing okay. I was much better now. I had my husband. As the night rolled in, we wanted to have some alone time. We somehow scraped up the money for a motel room. We got in his mom and dad's old car and took off. We went to sign in to get a room. They would not let us because neither of us had an ID. So now we went to one of Rick's friends to get a room for us. Then we were finally alone. We planned on just enjoying each other. Neither Rick nor I felt very content. This was not the best motel. The bed and sheets did not smell fresh. I remembered our bed back in Oklahoma. I longed for that security again. If we could just go back to the life we knew before. We knew that the world is not all that safe. I did not know that I would ever feel safe from this world. Every little noise made me jumpy. I wanted the security of my own bed, like my bed in Oklahoma. It was a strange place, and I knew it would take time to heal all these wounds.

It felt so good to be in Rick's arms again. I had been dreaming of this moment for years. We were now free to make our dreams come true. The night went so fast. I wanted to just stay there in Rick's arms forever. We were lying in bed, talking about everything, once again, making plans for our future. It seemed that the world had progressed without us. I could hear traffic and voices that did not sound familiar. I did feel safe lying in Rick's arms. But I knew we were still in Kern County. Then a knock came to the door. I jumped out of bed, looking for a place to hide, trying to find a way out. I really thought they were coming to get us. Who and why, I do not know. All I could think of was to hide and run when I got a chance. I knew now the cops could come and get you for nothing, say what they want to say about you, tear your family to pieces. Thank God this was not the law.

While Rick got the door, I was hiding in the bathroom. It was the motel's maid. She knew us and wanted to say hi. How did she know who we are? We checked in as Roberts. I hoped I get over this fast. I would hate to live my life afraid of my own shadow. Still excited to see our family, we rushed back over there to visit. Rick was ready for his mom's home-cooked breakfast. We all had so much to catch up on. Carol had a boyfriend, and little Lisa was not so little anymore. Carol was finishing up high school. She would graduate in June. Lisa would also graduate in June from eight grade. I wondered if my boys were going to school around here. I looked for them everywhere we go. Would I know them if I ran across them? Rick and I had set up a house in a camper in the backyard next door, next to Mom and Dad's. We fixed us a cozy little home for two. I loved playing house and cooking for my husband. Yes, he asked me to marry him again. He went back to work for the same man he worked for when this all began. We had been out a few days and decided it was time to go visit a few friends. I needed badly to see Colleen and Mom. The first stop we made, Gina was there. I was so glad to see her. We jumped up and down, hugging, crying, so happy to be free. This was so strange. It was like we were just plucked out of this world, and it moved on without us. Now we were back and had over six years of progress to catch up on.

Colleen's best friend Judy wanted to do something for Colleen and me. She said we were dressed out of date. So she took us on a whirlwind shopping spree. We shopped till we dropped. She bought us a whole new wardrobe. It was so much fun. We tried on so many things. We made a full day of it, and it was so much of what Colleen and I needed, a day out in the free world. I missed her a lot. The time went so fast. I missed spending time with Colleen. She stayed busy with her friends and family. Like us, she was trying to get her life back on the right path. I guess we were gone a little longer than we planned. Rick was so upset. He thought something had happened to us. This was the first time I had went anywhere without him. We had not got out of each other's sight. Colleen's life was moving fast, and I hoped she was up for it. She had already got both her daughters back. Windy was big and pregnant, and Amanda did not know we existed. She was twelve years old and a wild child. Amanda felt her whole life was a lie, and those around kept it going. I hoped she gave Colleen a chance to be a mother. She was young and needed a mother. We saw our girls a lot. They did not live with us, not yet anyway. We would get a home big enough for all of us. It felt so good being home. I saw the progress every day. I kept having a dream that my boys did not want me in their lives. All I could do was hope that they saw me on the news. I found myself looking for them—in the grocery stores, in the park. Every child I saw, I looked for them to be one of my boys. I listened for names to be called out. I believed I would know their voices, their walks. Would I even know them when I do see them? Being a mother, no matter how much time had passed, I would hope to know my own child. After all these years, there were so many changes in all our lives. They were no longer babies. I just did not know if I could handle rejection. I believed the right time would come, and I would be reunited with all three of my boys.

With every day that passed, that nightmare was further behind us. This first week had been very exciting. We had seen a lot of friends and family. I felt the world was moving so fast, and I was running to keep up with it. The only time I really felt safe was when Rick and I were locked in our little trailer, and I was wrapped in his arms. Life had been so hard on all of us and our children. The had been used by the courts, shuffled off to strange places, lied to, and made to lie while in court. It was not just the seven of us that had our lives stolen by the court system. They had also stolen the lives of our children. To lose their family and home at such a young age influenced lasting damage.

Now that we were home, maybe our children could live a happy ever after life. I still couldn't put away the fear of them coming after us again. I knew one thing, if Tommie found out I was home, he would find a way to get to me. I was not sure what to do. I wanted my children at home with me. I must be patient. Our day would come when the time was right. Rick and I wanted to remarry. We had it planned for after the holidays. Our wedding would be at the Knotty Pine, the place we met and fell in love, which felt like a life-time ago. Rick's aunt Ruleene gave me the money to go buy a dress to get married in. I was so full of joy looking for just that right dress. Lisa and a friend of hers went with me to the mall. We danced from store to store, looking for the perfect dress, giggling with the girls and cooing over all the pretty things through the mall. It was a good day that shattered all too quickly.

A lady hollered out to me, "Are you going to molest those girls also?" I couldn't even find the words to describe the way it made me feel. We would have to put up with this for the rest of our lives. My mood plummeted. It had occurred to me that even though we had won our appeal and found us innocent, there would be people like this lady that still believed those awful lies. I had just realized this would follow me throughout my life. To some people, it would not matter that I am innocent and have been cleared—not necessarily cleared. They said they could recharge us but did not have enough to retry us. Would this be held over my head for the rest of my life? I wanted to go back to Oklahoma as soon as I got my children back. I was free. I would learn to deal with it. People could think what they wanted. My children and the good Lord know the truth. I did not leave the house much after that. I went nowhere alone. You would think after the life I have lived, I would be a strong woman. I sup-posed I used it up. I knew I had a lot of healing to do. I knew time healed everything. I had been strong throughout all this misfortune that life has heaped upon me. Now that I was free, I still had a hard time dealing with life. I was a strong woman before all this. Time would heal me.

Christmas came faster than I expected. We had no money to buy gifts or decorations. But there was plenty of family and food. People were running in and out all day long. Our gift this year was freedom. On Christmas morning, as I sipped my coffee, I felt a real feeling of contentedness slipped over me. My boys were not here with me, maybe next year. But I was with my family, and I felt very loved.

As we started our new year, we also started our new life. Rick must go back to jail in March because of the joint he got caught within the prison. I was scared to death for him to leave me. I was not ready to be alone. He would only be about fifteen miles away, so I would get to visit him often. This seemed so unfair to me. At least he was going to jail for something he did do. He should not have to do more than a year. At least, I had my family to help me while he was gone. We wanted to remarry before he went back to jail. On January 12, 1991, I became Rick's wife again. The wedding was beautiful. The only thing missing was my three boys. How long must I wait? Rick's son Rickie was Rick's best man. Colleen was my maid of honor. The news crew was there. The place was packed with friends and families. My heart was beaming with love for the man I just went through hell with, back to the life we once had, sharing our wedding with the world, letting them know what the good Lord brings together no man can part—not even Kern County.

I had started to drive again, slowly gaining a little control over my life. I had been driving the girls to school just to spend some time with them. This world just kept spinning just as fast as it did the day I left prison. I just leaned into the curve and rolled with it. One day, I got a wonderful surprise. I was sitting over at Mom and Dad's house. I heard the gate open, the gate that separated us from the crazy world out. Also, that brought joy into our home. I looked to see who it was. It was my son, Tommie, my curly headed, blue-eyed baby. We ran to each other's arm for a crushing hug. I had waited so long for this, the first of my babies to come home to his momma. While walking hand in hand, he told me that he had seen on the news that his momma was home. I guess having our wedding on TV did serve a purpose. He came to find me. I knew he would come looking for me the minute he found out I was home. He did not run from his father's house. Tommie had escaped from the juvenile facility. He told them he was sick and needed to go to the hospital. He ran the first chance he got. It hurt me that my son had been lock up as I had been. That was what the courts have done for him. They taught them to lie and took him from his mother. They brought doubt to his mind that his mother no longer loved him. If I would get to raise my sons, maybe, just maybe, he might have had a chance at a good life. I told him we had to do the right thing and go back. If we did not take him back, he and I both would be in trouble with the law. Once again, the courts would separate us. So now when he got out, he could come live with Momma. It was hard taking him back. I sure did not trust the law. I was afraid they would trump up something else on me. It was terrible that I must live this way. Those who we were supposed to trust to serve and protect us were the very ones that had already torn my world apart. We called the press before we called the sheriff's department to come get Tommie just to make sure they did not make up more lies about us. He did get to keep in touch with me when he was up at Camp Owens. We also got to go see him a couple of times. It was a camp for boys that got in trouble. The stories of his life—Tommie just couldn't stay out of trouble. Things might have been different if I could have been there to raise him. Now he probably would get in more trouble for his escape. He just wanted to see his momma.

I tried not to think about Rick having to go back to jail. I must paint my smile on somedays as the time got closer and closer for Rick to leave me and go do his time. We had intel on the twelfth of March, and I planned on spending every minute I could with him. I got me a part-time job, waitressing at Knotty Pine. I had been going on the truck with him when I do not have to work. Rick had been driving to Los Angeles and back a couple of times a day. That was a beautiful ride from Bakersfield. He loved being a truck driver. The beauty started your spirit soaring. We were just listening to country music, talking about our new lives together, the past and the future. Sometimes, we were quiet, just enjoying the beauty before us. I thank the good Lord for giving us our life back, praying our family finds it way together once again. Rick knew I was having a hard time adjusting to this world we live in. He was trying to save a little money for me to take care of myself while he was gone. I would just have to stay strong. It was not like it was the first time I had been on my own. I did it then, and I would do it now. I would miss him and the moments we share like this one and all the wonderful things ahead of us. Just a short hold up and he would be gone and back before I knew it.

The lawyers did not end with the winning of our appeal. Now they were calling us about filing a civil suit against Kern County. They should not be allowed to do this to anyone else. They should pay for what they have done to our children and us. Three hundred and seventy-three years sounded good to me. I was not sure if I could go back and relive the hell we had already been through. We all got together and talked to the kids. We asked them if they were ready to tell our side of this story. I did not want to do this if they were not up to it. We had already been through a lot of pain. We all agreed this is what we would do—take on Kern County. I told the kids it was our turn to tell the truth, to let the world know what this county has done to us. Stan Berker was our lawyer. He said this would all take some time. I was going to put this all behind me for now and concentrate on getting my life together. I was full on board with getting back at Kern County. Someone should pay for what they did to our children and us. I told my children it would make us all feel better with all these lies behind us.

Clovette and Cliff, they still had warrants out for their arrest. Cliff came out to get everything cleared. Cliff and his family had been hiding out in Georgia for the last couple of years. Clovette and the kids stayed in Georgia till they know everything is cleared. For six long years, Cliff would move with the wind if they even thought someone has found out who there are. Hopefully, after today, their running was over. We all got together, piled up in Mike Pitts's van, and headed to the courthouse. Once again, we called the press for protection against Kern County. If anything came up, it would hit the five o'clock news. There must have been ten or more of us. We walked in there, putting all our fears behind us. Cliff walked up to the warrant window, asking if there was a warrant out for Clifford or Clovette Pitts. When the clerk finally returned, we were all gathered up to hear what she had to say. She said all charges had been dropped. We cried with happy tears, whooping with joy. Their life of being hunted like an animal was finally over. We all ran to get back to the van. We were trying to ditch the press.

As we all piled in the van, one of the news guys piled in with us. All we could tell him was we were all free now and trying to fit into this world that is all new to us. Everything had changed. The children we knew were almost grown. Cliff had been on the run with his family for more than six long years. Now we were all free with no more threats, free to settle down and live our lives wherever we choose. Clover had been my best friend for most of my life. I couldn't wait to see Clover. I had misses her so very much.

March 12 came way too fast. It was time for Rick to go back to jail. He must do one year in a lardo. Our niece Amanda wanted to go to court with us, so I did not have to go alone. I thought maybe taking her to the courthouse would not be a good thing. She had absolutely had no memory of ever being at a courthouse. She had no memory of any of the things she has been through. She wanted to see her uncle Rick off. She had always loved us very much. Amanda and I were sitting outside the courtroom, waiting to see what happens to Rick. The courtroom was too full, so we could not go in. Walking up the hallway, coming our way was one of our trial attorneys, Mike Vandrosco. He walked right up to me and said, "Marcella, I am so glad to see you out." With just those few words, I knew this man had known the truth all along. Hearing my name rolled off that man's lips again brought a chill to the bones. He would not have said that if he did not know we were innocent. What is wrong with these people? Amanda, like her mother, read the look on my face. I was fixing to give this man a piece of my mind. Amanda jumped and said, "I guess you know who I am. I am Amanda Bennett." He looked at her and just walked away. They would go to hell for what they put our children through. I would always believe they knew the truth all along. Now I was on my own. Rick was not here for me to lean on. Not sure how long he would be gone. I must be strong and not let the world know that I am still shaking on the inside. I stayed in my little trailer most of the time. My best friend Yvonne talked me into moving in with them till Rick comes home. I felt much safer in our little trailer. I believed it was time for me to get over my fears and face what life threw at me.

Rick's aunt and uncle were taking a trip to Georgia to visit their son. They asked me if I would like to go with them so I could see Clovette. I could not turn them down. I needed so badly to see my big sister. It had been almost seven years since I had seen her. I needed to see her so I would know she is okay. I would look into her eyes, see her smile, and hug her tightly. Then I would know she is going to be fine. Rick wanted me to wait till he got home. I needed to see my sister. I could not turn them down. The ride from California to Georgia was the most beautiful magical ride I have ever been on. There were so many different colors of green—the beauties of this earth, the trees, the stars, the rivers, and lakes, all so incredibly beautiful. It brought tears to my eyes. I had been looking at those old gray walls for so long. Now the walls of my little secure trailer were what I see. I was wondering if I would ever get to see these beautiful places again. I had forgotten the beautiful things the good Lord has given us to enjoy while we spend our time here on this earth. It was if I was seeing it all for the first time. I would never take the world's beauties for granted again. The world we live in is filled with its natural beauties. Only man can take that away.

I was so nervous when we pulled up at Clovette's. Would she know who I am? We were seven years older now. Both of us had gone through pure hell. When we pulled in their driveway, I felt like a child again. I was overwhelmed with excitement. I could not wait to see my big sister. The door flew open, and here she came, flying into my arms. We were wiping each other's tears. We were laughing, crying, and catching up on many missed hugs. Finally, I was with my sister and her family that I have missed for so long. We sat at the kitchen table and shared our experiences of the last seven years. It was so hard on them, running from state to state with two children. It was just wonderful seeing Clover and her family. I had missed her so very much.

Her kids were not little anymore. I couldn't even imagine what they had been through, running and hiding your identity from everyone you meet, always afraid the FBI would be right on their trail. For the first couple of years, they were on their trail. Being on the run must have been terrible, not knowing from one day to the next if they were going to catch up with you and take your babies away. They had been going through their own kind of hell. We sat for hours, telling story after story. Clover's worst fear was that Kern County would catch up with them and take her children. She told me there were times she wished she were with us because she missed us so bad. She was bitter, and the answer to all problems was to have another beer. I think she might drink a little too much. Maybe now that all charges were dropped, they could get their life back in order. Hopefully, time would also heal my sister. I spent a wonderful week with Cliff and Clover and their children. Our time together went so fast. I did not like being so far from Rick. I was ready for the long, beautiful ride home. This world might be scary, but it was also beautiful. I enjoyed the ride home as much as the ride there. Rick's aunt Ruleene and uncle Troy were wonderful people, and I loved spending time with them. Now it was back to the real world. With Rick locked up again, I now stood alone.

When I got back, it was time for me to get my life together. The visit with Clover was just what I needed to motivate myself. Her life had been torn to shreds. She was the one I have always looked up to. Now I would try to be a good role model. Maybe that would motivate her. Time to hold my head high and take on the world. Time to go to work. First stop, Knotty Pine café. I was hired on the spot. For some reason, I always went there first. I guess that place was a part of me. I felt comfortable and at ease there. I knew most of their customers. They were the same people that came in when Rick's parents ran it. I loved my job there. It kept me busy—not a lot of time to think about what had happened to us. Then the boss lady told me that Lisa couldn't come down while I was working because it made her boys fight. Lisa had been coming to that place all her life. I quit. It had never been hard for me to find a job. This time it was a little different. It seemed I have lost my confidence. I was afraid people would know who I am and where I have been. This was a fear I felt every time I walked in or out a door. I just couldn't sit here and wait on Rick to take care of me. I had always stood on my own, and I would continue to do so. I did find me a job, working in a slim motel. This was not the work I prefer, but it would pay the bills till Rick comes home to me. Mom had always told me, "Work hard and take care of yourself. You cannot always count on someone else to take care of your needs." I must take care of myself. Living with Yvonne and Ang made it much easier for me. I did not want to come home to an empty house. I got to see Rick once a week. The first visit was the worst. It was hard on me walking into that jail. I had a fear of Kern County's sheriff officers. If I was in their facility, they might not let me out. I was always thinking, *This is a trap*. I walked in there. It was because my love for Rick was stronger than fear. They imposed upon me—another thing that would pass with time. When Rick got out of there, if I never see another jail, it would be too soon for me. I had seen enough jails for a lifetime. A few people were trying to get Rick out early. I hoped it works. I needed him home with me. I knew this was hard on him. I also knew he had an out date.

A friend of ours came over to see me. She said one of her nieces went to school with my oldest son Johnnie. She wanted to know if I would like to send him a massage. Of course, I did. I was not sure what to say. I wrote a long letter then tore it up. So I made it simple, and to the point, I wrote him a note and told him, "My dearest John boy, I love you very much, son, and if you ever want to see me, I will be waiting on your call." I put a couple of numbers where I could be reached. With shaking hands, I put my note in an envelope and sealed it. I also said a prayer for the good Lord to reunite me with my son. I lay awake most of the night, wondering if my firstborn son would call me or throw my note away. The next day, he tried to get ahold of me. I missed the first couple of calls. I waited for the phone to ring. When I answered, he said tentatively, "Momma?" My heart leaped. I would know that voice anywhere. Johnnie, my oldest son, was seventeen years old at the time. It was wonderful to hear his voice again. He must have called me about ten times that day.

He said, "Momma, I am afraid I will call this number, and you will not be there." I promised him I would never go away again. He said, "Mom, should we wait till I turn eighteen to come see you?" I told him it was up to him, whatever made him feel comfortable. He said, "I do not want you to get in trouble." No one had told me not to see my boys. I was willing to take the chance. We said good night several times and a whole bunch of I love you and miss you. I did believe I had just started healing from all this lingering pain. "Momma," I love hearing that, and I believed my son enjoyed saying it. I could have stayed on the phone with him all night. But I did not. My face hurt from smiling. I believed we were on the road to recovery. We would all be reunited very soon. I was up early the next morning, sitting at the table, having me some coffee, smiling. I loved my life. It was finally coming together. If only Rick was here to share it. The phone rang, and it was Johnnie calling me. He had called five or six times just to make sure it was really me and told me he loved me. I was so happy that I cried, and I laughed. I knew this was not a dream. It was a dream come true. No, we did not wait till Johnnie was eighteen. He called me back later that day. He was ready to meet up with me.

We set it up to meet at Burger King that afternoon. I pulled in and parked. I saw him standing by the Bugger King door. I could see him from my rearview mirror. I just watched him for a long moment, taking in one deep breath then another. He searched the face of every person that came his way. Yes, I did recognize my firstborn son as he was standing in the doorway, looking for his momma. He was not a little boy anymore. I could not sit in my car another minute. Finally, I got out of the car, slamming the car door behind me. As he heard the door slam, his eyes flashed my way. I slowly started walking in his direction. I saw a big smile come across his face, and the word that came next was "Momma." We both started running to each other. My firstborn son was right there in the Burger King driveway. I was not sure if the hug lasted for seconds or minutes. We hugged and hugged again. I never wanted to let him go. I wanted to stop time and hug my son forever. We were both crying, but this time it was happy tears. I told him just how much I have loved and missed him and his brothers. I told him about Tomboy escaping to see me. He said, "Sounds like Tommie."

I sat there and listened to the stories that my son was telling me. I did not bring up anything about where I had been and the hard life. I had endured without them. I would wait till they wanted to talk about things. He told me about his life. He no longer lived with his dad. He lived with his girlfriend. He was thrown out of his house. They threw him out like the daily trash. I am sure there was a reason for this. I just did not understand why my children have all live apart. I guess time would fill me in. I had now seen two of my boys and now to see my baby Bryan. Johnnie said when the time was right, he would get Bryan and me together. We talked for a while, and I was going to come get him tomorrow. We had so much to catch up on. I had waited so long for this. It was hard to say goodbye. This was not goodbye. It was "I will see you tomorrow." I had missed him so very much.

The phone was ringing when I got home from work. I rushed into the house to answer. It was Johnnie calling. He said, "Momma, someone wants to talk to you." I thought maybe it was his girlfriend checking out his story that his momma was home. If my Johnnie loved her, so would I. I was wrong. I heard my baby Bryan say, "Momma." This was a breath of fresh air. I wish there were words to explain the way I feel. He said, "I want to see my momma." We were going to meet up tomorrow. I couldn't wait to go see Rick and tell him all the good things going on. Bryan and I were having our stolen moments once again. He said he did not want his father to know yet. No one had ever told me not to see them. I let them come to me whenever they wanted, just like I knew they would. Now all three of my boys had made it truly clear they wanted me in their lives. My soul had been broken, which I thought was unrepairable. I could not be healed without my children. Now the healing could begin. The courts might laugh at me, and I did not care. I promised my boys I would never stop fighting for them.

When I went on my next visit with Rick, I told him about the boys. He was incredibly pleased. He told me to slow down when it comes to Bryan. He did not want me in trouble. He said when I came home, we would go back to court and get the boys, just like we tried to seven years ago. Johnny turned eighteen and moved in with me. Bryan and I continued seeing each other daily. I even went up to his school and met his teachers. He said, "This is my mom." She said not his birth mother. We both laughed and said yes. She did not know what to think—no telling what she had been told about me. Johnnie, Bryan, and I spent a lot of time catching up on each other's life. My poor babies, they had been through six years of hell by themselves. They said their house had never been a happy home. They told me their stepmother was not genuinely nice to them. She fought with them over any little thing. Tommie said she would beat them for getting a glass of milk—any reason she could find to punish them and keep them in their room. Johnnie said he went to bed hungry many nights. That was her way of punishing them. He also told me she broke his nose when she caught him with a girlfriend at church. She and Tommie never did see eye to eye. He said, "Mom, I was her punching bag. She hated me." He left home at an early age, started getting in trouble, and was not allowed to go home by his father and stepmother, who wanted my boys so badly. They took my son to a judge and said they did not want him. My children needed me as badly as I needed them. If I could just get Tommie and Rick home, I would do my absolute best to give my husband and my children a happy home.

It seemed to me that while my family was fighting for our lives, our children were fighting for their lives too. I was trying so hard to hold things together. All I ever wanted was to have my boys and Rick and the girls all together so we could be a happy family. That is when we all were the happiest when we were all together before all this began. Johnnie and Lisa both lived with me now. Bryan was here most of the time. I felt like we were crowding Yvonne and Angela out. I told her when Rick got home, we would move. Yvonne loved us and loved that my family was slowly coming together.

We were having a family reunion, and Rick and Tommie were not home yet. My dad and his wife were coming. Clovette and Cliff and their three children were coming in from Georgia. Yvonne was letting us have our family and friends reunion at her house. This would be a blast. It would be the first time we had all been together in seven years or longer. My father was the happiest father alive, having all four of his children and grandchildren home again. I loved seeing our family laughing, joking, getting to know about each other's life. We had all missed so much of each other. I looked around at our children, remembering when they were all babies, and now they were all teenagers. Our lives moved on so very fast. Now we would build a new life and share it with each other. We had a good turnout. People were coming and going all day long. We were seeing a lot of our old friends and family for the first time since we came home. Johnnie, Bryan, Carol, and Lisa were all there with me. I was so proud to have most of my family with me. We were missing Rick and Tomboy. They would both be home soon. My mom and dad, almost all my children, my four siblings, and their families were all there. I was the happiest I had been in a long time. My face was sore from smiling. We all had a wonderful time. When it was all over, it was time for the family to head home. A feeling of loneliness came over me. I loved my family very much, Rick's family as well. I would love to have a family reunion every weekend. But we all lived so far apart. Hopefully, it would not always be this way.

Holding Things Together

I had heard that Rick was coming up for sheriff's parole. If he got it granted, he could come home early. This was getting harder every day for me to hold things together. I would not change it for the world. I believe my hands were filling up fast. I needed my husband home. When they took my babies from me, they were babies. Now they were all teenagers. I did not know how to do this. I thought all we had to do was be together, and everything would be all right. Whoever said life is easy? I did not like my job. I would find another one when Rick gets home. We had three teenagers living here, and Bryan was here whenever he could get by with it. Holding things together was not easy. I did not think I was being a good mother. I was so afraid they would get mad at me and leave me again. I just couldn't say no. They were running all over me. Yvonne worked during the night, and I worked during the day so one of us would be home with the kids. Johnnie was eighteen now and did not listen to a word I say. He was not making the right decisions in his life. I did not bring us all together so we could fall apart together. I prayed for strength and guidance that I do not fall apart here. Johnnie stayed out for days at a time. I could tell he was using drugs. He was doing all the wrong things. I had failed him in some way. Being a good mother is not as easy when you hold on to the fear of losing them again. Johnnie also quit school. He was eighteen now and could do what he wanted.

Rick just called and said he believed they turned him down for sheriff's parole. That is sure not what I wanted to hear. I needed him home so badly. I was falling apart here, and I couldn't seem to stop it. Could I hold it together till he gets home?

About that time, the phone rang. A friend of ours said, "Is he there yet?" They had granted Rick the sheriff's parole. He was coming home. I ran in Yvonne's room, jumping up and down, saying he is coming home. I ran outside, and there he was, walking down the street to our house. I went running down the street to my husband's arms. Finally, he was home and should never have to leave me again. Now we could work on a full house together. Life was changing for us every day. I was so glad my husband was here and by my side to help me with all this life's choices. I had been trying so hard to bring my family back together. Holding it there was the problem. Rick had gone back to work, driving a truck. We went to get a lawyer. Bryan wanted to come home, and Tommie wanted to come home when he gets out of Camp Owens. Bryan had been giving his dad pure hell. When his father found out he was seeing me, he was not incredibly happy about it. Bryan believed if he fought with his dad, it would be his way out, and he could come home to us. We were having problems making him go to school. His dad sent him to school, and he was on the bus to my house. I wanted him here also, but we must go to court first, and he needed to go to school. I was so glad Rick was home. He was stricter than I am. I supposed all fathers were. We got a lawyer and court date for custody of Tommie and Bryan. Johnnie was already living with us. I already saw that it was going to be a job getting our lives backtrack. Just being together did not fix anything.

Our court hearing on the boys came fast, unlike the first one that seemed to take forever, and they took my boys from me. On the morning of court, we all marched down there together. Rick, Carol, Lisa, Johnnie Jr., Bryan, and I all went to the courthouse. We were all here to fight for the family that should have never been a part in the first place. When I came upon Johnnie Martin Sr., I had to ask him why he let this happen. He knew my family and me very well, and he also knew this never happened. I told him he knew we were good people. He replied, "I had to believe my boys." That was just not a satisfying answer. I guess I would never know why or how this happened. There was no fight this time. Johnnie said I could have my boys. That simple. He just handed them over to me. He had really been having trouble with each of them and did not want to deal with it anymore. Of course, they were having trouble. Look at what they had been through. They had a terrible stepmother that did not like them, a father that did not pay attention to what was going on with his children. My boys had told me stories about their stepmother. The abuse she made them suffer till she left their house while their father turned a blind eye. I was giving it my all to pick up the pieces of my broken family. She was the one that should go to prison. She had abused my children for years. The boys were so full of anger and distrust. I did not know if I would ever get through to them. I loved them all so very much, and now I was starting to realize that love might not be enough. Every night when I went to bed, I thanked the good Lord above for bringing us together again. If only I could just find the strength to keep us together. I felt like I was not being the best mom at this point in my life. I did not want them mad at me. I was afraid they would leave and not come back.

We had moved into our own house. I was so grateful to Yvonne and Ang for putting up with us while we pulled our family together again. Tommie would be coming home soon—one step closer to having all my children home. We were working on a full house. Johnnie had an accident at work right before we got out of prison. He messed up his hand badly. He had a couple of surgeries on it, and he used it as an excuse to not do anything. I couldn't get him up for school. He did not want to go to work. We had been going to therapy for a while, and they said he had 95 percent use of his hand. I also thought he was doing drugs. We gave him a choice to go to work or school or move out. So he moved in and out till things got bad. Drugs had taken him over. This was coming in between Rick and me and him and Rick. Johnnie kept a rather good eye on me. I knew with all my heart that Johnnie loved me. My children did not love their selves. His life had been so messed up that he did not know how to act. He said to me one day, "Mom, the drugs numb me." I always told him how much I love him and how I have missed him while I was away. I did not know what to do. How do I help my children?

Rick and I had decided to reopen the Knotty Pine, the place where our love began. The last people that leased it tore it up. Rick's mom and dad still owned it. We had a lot of work ahead of us.

Hopefully, this would be a family business. My sister Colleen and her boyfriend and Rick's brother Cliff helped us remodel. We worked in that place for months. On April 6, 1992, we opened the doors to the Knotty Pine Café. I still got overwhelmed when I am around people. I must work on trying to trust people again. Our little place was a great success. The hard work and the kids kept me busy. No one knew how I felt inside. I tried my best to cover it up. I had always felt like the Knotty Pine was a good part of me. I felt so unsure of myself as a mother and a wife. Colleen and Gina both worked for us. I felt best when we were all together. They both seemed to be doing good, getting their lives back together. Either that or like me, they were holding it all inside.

Between the kids and the Knotty Pine, I stayed busy—too busy to cry. I was falling apart out here, and nobody knew but me. I did not even know why I cry. Was it the life that had gone and passed or just my life that seemed to fit together like broken glass? I thought after all we have been through, life would be easy—happily ever after, like in the movies. Raising teenagers was not so easy. They had no respect for anyone. Kern County had damaged my children. I would not ever give up on any one of them. I did good when Rick was with me. Like my children, I was lost, and I couldn't find the strength to keep strong. I must get a grip on myself. My children needed me. Kern County authorized them to lie and be deceitful. That was what they knew. I was pushing through this, and soon I would see everything would work out. I thought after I got out of prison, life would magically fall into place. Each puzzle piece fit just like before. I had found that none of the pieces fit, no matter how I tried to glue them together.

Lisa and Bryan were in high school now, getting more independent every day. Carol stayed busy with school and her boyfriend. She did not have much time for us. Sometimes, I thought she did not like us, or was it herself she did not like? When I looked in her eyes, I saw pain and anger. She was once a carefree child, and Kern County had taken that away from her. She was so smart and beautiful and now full of sorrow. I did not know if we would ever get over this. We were all trying to adjust to each other. Time would heal. Carol asked for a cooking job at the Knotty Pine. She was out of school for spring break. Carol was in her freshman year of college. She never went back to school. She continued working at the Knotty Pine.

Tommie finally made it home. He had spent most of the last five years locked up. When he was nine years old, he got into it with his stepmother. He hit her and did his first six months locked up. He carried much more anger than the other children. He had almost done as much time as I had. No one could ever understand Tommie like I did. No one can love your child like a mother does.

Tommie was seventeen now and very used to making his own rules. I told him just like we told Johnnie, "Work or school?" We enrolled him at North High with Lisa and Bryan. Rick was out on the truck, and the kids were a hand full, ditching school, doing what they wanted, not listening to Mom. The Knotty Pine was a lot of work and a full-time job. The stress was just growing. Things were not good at home. Rick had lost his interest in me. Lisa had moved back in with her mother. Johnnie was strung on drugs, living here and there. Tommie moved out and was running with Johnnie—both on meth. Now we just had Bryan at home. I felt like I had failed as a mother. I was so bruised that I couldn't help my children. I was so afraid of losing them again. I just did things wrong. I did not want to lose my boys or my husband. I wanted to be a mother and a wife to Rick. The more I tried, the more I lost. Love brought us back together. But love was just not enough to hold us that way.

Rick's parents were moving back to Oklahoma. This gave us a little financial relief. We were going to move into their house. It was smaller, but our family was not as big as it should be. The three of us got busy. We cleaned it up, painted it, and made us a nice little home. It had a big backyard. We could plant a garden if we wanted to. I was still having a hard time. I had tried to talk to Rick, and he said to stop dwelling on the past. How do I stop when it is all around me every day? I guess he just did not understand me. It was not only the past. It was the past few weeks—the past couple of months trying so hard to bring my family back together. Yes, the past had damaged me. This world had whipped me, but I would never give up on our children or my marriage. My love was just not good enough to hold this family together. I just couldn't love away what Kern County had done to all of us. About that time, I thought it could not get worse. I guess I should not have tempted fate. For now, it had all came to a boil.

The Knotty Pine was broken into. They broke open the safe and stole all our cash. This was one of our busiest nights. We had a pool league dinner. When we called the police, they came out to investigate. We realized we know who did this. It was Johnnie and Tommie. The police officer said it was a family dispute, and we should handle it ourselves. Things were falling apart. Rick was prowling this town, looking for my boys. Of course, this caused problems for Rick and me. After all we had been through, why did we come against each other? Bryan was running around with his brothers and was getting into trouble. If that is what you look for, that is what you get. He was using drugs with his brothers. I did not know what kind, but I could tell. He just was not acting right. No one was acting right. We were all so messed up. Bryan got kicked out of school. I pleaded with them to let him go to school. They would not have it, so I put him in school at the juvenile hall. Bryan began to lie and kept stealing things from our house—Rick's guns, our stereo, money.

I felt that my life was slowly falling apart one day at a time. I was not sure what to do. My sister Clovette said, "Send him to me. I am tougher than you." All we could do was give it a try. My baby Bryan went to Georgia. His uncle Cliff said that if he did not go to school, he would put him to work. I had to get him away from his brothers. Separating them was all I know to do. All my children had gone away. Would my heart ever stop breaking? I still saw Johnnie and Tommie running the streets. They were living nearby, so I still got to see them. This was so hard to watch my babies like this. Johnnie's girlfriend was going to have a baby. I believed she was also using drugs. I tried so hard to hold my family together. It had fallen apart faster than the sand that slipped right through my fingers.

We grew further apart every day. My house was no longer too small. It was down to Rick and me, and we seemed to be pushing each other away. I had struggled so hard to get my family back together. Now I watched it fell apart one person at a time. Now if I only could hold my marriage together. I did not think Rick was in love with me anymore. I knew he loved me, but I did not think he was in love with me. Prison had changed all of us. Rick held it all in acts as if it never happened. He hardened his heart. I did understand why he did not want my boys around. I just couldn't give up on them. I was their mother, and life had not been so good to us. I would not give up on being a mother or a wife to Rick. I would make him love me again. After all we had been through, we couldn't let this come between us.

I tried to keep busy at the Knotty Pine. It kept me from dwelling. I had a lot of friends, and I felt so alone in this life. I felt like a teenager that no one understands. Life was not easy to get back into. I was struggling here, and no one seemed to notice. I talked to my mom as much as I could. Her voice still calmed me. She was doing okay. She was staying with Aunt Peggy, her sister. A couple of hours away, Colleen was also having hell with her girls. Windy gave birth to a beautiful baby girl Shelby. Amanda was on the run, doing whatever she could get by with. I moved Amanda in with me, hoping Rick and I could get a grip on her. It did not work. She would take off two or three days at a time. I gave her back to her mother. Kern County should have offered us some counseling. The good Lord knows we all needed it.

I had started drinking a lot more. It numbed my pain. The tears, I just couldn't hold back anymore. I cried at the drop of a hat. This was so hard on me, and it felts like no one cares. I was drowning here, and it was only getting worse. All Rick said was "Get over it." I wish I could. I could see he was frustrated with me. When I got out of prison, I never thought I could feel this way again. This is not the way it was supposed to turn out. We were going to live happily ever after. What went wrong? I did not have my family back. I did not have my life back. Rick and I were young and so in love, we thought we could conquer the world. Now I had problems conquering each day. It felt like I had a bundle of shards. The more I tried, the more I got cut.

Just about that time, I thought I could not get worse. Here came the holidays. We were having a party at the Knotty Pine. The sadness came over me, and I did not want to live another day. I left the party and never planned to come back again. When I got in the car, I saw my niece's and nephew's Christmas presents. I wanted to get them to them. It was a bit early, but I did not want to be around to see Christmas. When I went over there, those kids showed me just how much they loved me. They adored me. I was their aunt Tootie. Their father was my brother Wayne. He was a mess, and he was that way before any of this and continued to be a mess now. His wife Carol did a good job of holding things together while Wayne was in prison. This woke me up. It was enough to change my way of thinking. What was I thinking? I was loved and needed in this world. I just couldn't believe I let myself get this down and depressed. I was not weak. I was a strong woman. The world had knocked me down, and I would never let something like this take me over again. It was not only hard on me, but I saw sis and Gina struggling also. Mom just rolled with the flow. It was her body that failed her. She had a bad fall and was in the hospital for a while. She was coming home to live with Colleen. It would be nice to have Mom around again. She was not really healthy. It seemed we had all picked up our lives. Now if we could only just get the pieces to come together. I never dreamed my boys would leave me again. I felt so broken. I loved Rick very much, and I would try to make it work for us. Rick made it home most weekends. I might be wrong, but I did not believe he was at work when he was not home on the weekends. I would not give up till I got it right.

The Knotty Pine was thriving. It was a good little business. I wish I could give it my all. I did not know where my all was. I had let the world damage me. I just did not understand why I couldn't just be happy and be satisfied with what I have. I had made lots of good memories at the Knotty Pine, and I wanted to make many more. Johnnie and Tommie had both made their way to jail over drugs. We had missed out on so much. It looked like we would miss out a lot more. Johnnie and Crystal had a new baby boy right before he went to jail. That was one of the most exciting times in my life, to watch my first blood grandson be born. We named him Johnnie III. I loved being a mother, and I loved being a grandmother as well.

Civil Suit

The time had come for us to try to make this county pay for what they had done to our children and us. The first thing we did wrong is all of us used the same attorney—one guy, six of us, and Kern County. Here we go again. First off, picked jury. Our families were scattered all over. Tomboy was in prison, and Johnnie was out but on the run from his parole officer. I hoped maybe this civil suit was healing for us. I knew we would at least have our say. My niece Christina was coming out from Georgia to testify in this trial. Lisa, Amanda, and Bryan did not remember any of what happened to us. Wayne, my brother, got caught with some drugs, and our lawyer dropped him from the case. I did not agree with that. To me, it was just one more thing to blame on Kern County. My family would forever feel the pain that remains in our hearts. So now there were five of us. Not sure why Wayne F. was not here with us. Windy was strung out on drugs and did not want to go through it again. Once again, she did not want to feel life. "Drugs are the only way to cope with life" was what she said. Just look at what they had done to my family. We let our lawyer had our house, and we moved in at the Knotty Pine. We were trying to save the lawyer a little money just to tell this suit is over. We knew this would take a while but surely not as long the criminal trial.

I was wrong. This did not help us. I told Carol it would make us feel better if we got the chance to get up on that stand and tell the world what we have been through. Carol got up there on that stand, and that tore her apart again—just like in the trial. She looked at me and said, "You lied to me." I told her it would not be like the trial. Nothing had changed. Now I wish we would not have had this civil suit. We brought Tommie in from prison to testify. When they brought him into the courtroom, the jangling sound sent from his chains sent shivers down my spine. He was young and did not remember a lot. It was so hard on me seeing my son up there on that stand with chains on his foot just like we had during our trial. The main thing he did remember was that this crap never happened. He remembered Andy Gindes yelling at him and throwing things against the wall then slamming out of the room, leaving him in that room all alone. They were scared of not saying the things he wanted him to say. That would scare any child. Johnny came to testify and was arrested right after he got off the stand—validation of his probation. This was not so easy—rehashing all this sick stuff again. If we had healed, this would surely be a step backward. This was reopening wounds that have never healed.

Every day, we went back to Knotty Pine for lunch. I spent that hour crying my eyes out. Why did we do this again? This trial was no different. We got up there and tried to defend ourselves. They still made us look like liars. Christina finally made it out and testified. She told them she tried to tell them that nothing like that had ever happened to her. After fifty visits from the district attorney's office, she said they finally broke her—forced to lie. Chris was all grown up and had a baby of her own. I hated what was happening to our family again.

We should have had five lawyers up there fighting, not one taking this crap from Kern County. I was not handling this very well. Seeing my boys like this was hard on me. Johnnie and Tommie both were having such a hard time with life. They both wanted to keep themselves numbed up with drugs. They told me, "It is hard to feel anything when you have hurt your mother like we have." I had told them time and time again, none of this was their fault. This civil suit was pulling my heart and stomping on it. We had Andy Gindes on the stand. He or no one else would admit they were in the wrong. I just shut this hearing right out of my mind. I was here, but I tried to keep my mind somewhere else. I just couldn't take any more. We were once again devastated. Of course, we lost again. They found that Gindes, the district attorney, Vandrosco, assistant district attorney, the darlings investigators had absolute prosecutorial immunity.

Andy Gindes's immunity, the appeals court found over five hundred counts of prosecutorial misconduct. How could he be found not accountable for what he has done to us? Not one person would admit what they have done to many people. How could they sleep at night? I knew one thing for sure at the end of our life here on earth, we all had the same judge. Now the state of California charged Rick and me $314,000 for court cost. For this, I had the chance to watch the court system covered their ass and play as they have done no wrong again. Mom, Colleen, and Gina were all on assistance. They could not be charged. No win again. Now we wait on another appeal. I would not hold my breath on that one. I was so glad this part of our life was over. Why would I think for one minute we would get some justice out of good oh Kern County? I was glad this was finally over. I felt so relieved. I just wanted to put that part of my life behind me. I did not even want justice anymore. I knew they would never pay for what they had done to many families. It was futile. I just wanted to never have to look at those smiling devil face again.

Moving On

The Knotty Pine had slowed way down. Not sure if it was the court hearings or the fact Rick and I rarely get along. I had known for a while now that Rick was seeing someone else, a family friend. With friends like that, one did not need enemies. Now that everyone else knew, it was harder for me to act like it was not happening. I just couldn't be the happy little wife. We fought about my boys all the time. Rick was not the same man I married in 1984. He had hardened. Now he had moved out. He moved back down to Knotty Pine. I must be getting used to the pain. My boys did not stick around, and now my husband had moved out. My best friend Yvonne got married and moved about four hours away. It sure was lonely at home all alone. I felt like a broken woman. I tried to be a good mother and wife. I worked hard to keep the Knotty Pine going. Life again was wearing me down. I did believe I give a dam is busted. I just lay around, feeling sorry for myself. I got where I did not want to go home.

But spending time over at Colleen's house showed me every one of us had a messed-up life. My house was a mess, and my laundry was piled high. I knew this was just life. Rick and I had been seeing a lot of each other. We couldn't seem to let go. I hated it that he had moved out. I finally asked him to move home. He took me up on it and moved back home and promised to never cheat again. I still could not trust him, and I questioned his every move. I am sure it would take time. It was up to him to make me trust him again. I had made us both miserable. An exceptionally good friend of ours asked me to go to Las Vegas with her. She said she needed to talk to me. She picked me up at the house—no small talk, no questions. We were quiet the entire four-hour ride to Vegas. It was nice and peaceful. Judy did not talk all the way there. When we got to our room, she said, "I brought you to talk to you about you and Rick." She went on to say she was there to watch us fall in love and there to see us go through hell and back, which only made me stronger. She said that we were hurting everyone that loves us. Both of our families are suffering over this. She said, "Suck it up and save your marriage or just move on." Rick and I talked all night on the phone. We had decided to fight for our marriage. We had the rest of our lives to make this marriage work. I was in for the duration. I just could not see life without Rick by my side. We closed the doors of the Knotty Pine. I would miss it, but it would be a good miss. It was too much for me anyway.

All our kids were doing their own thing. Johnny and Tommie were in and out of prison, and Bryan was in Georgia, working with his uncle Cliff. Lisa moved to Oklahoma. Rick's parents, Cliff and Norma, let Lisa and her boyfriend lived with them. They were having a baby in May. I knew Rick's parents loved having Lisa there. A new baby—I was so excited. Carol did not come around much. She was busy with her life. Johnnie's girlfriend had another baby, a sweet baby girl, Chelsea. She looked just like her daddy. I still spent my days missing my boys. The three little boys that met me at the bingo hall were forever gone. I did not know the people they had grown up to be. I mourned for the three little boys they took from me so many years ago. Colleen's little granddaughter Shelby was a shining star in our lives. She loved going on the truck with Rick and me. It was a big adventure for her. It also gave her a break from the Hackett life her grandmother lived. Colleen might be a grandmother, but not even that slowed her down. Her life was very hectic. Shelby's mother Windy, like my boys, had no direction, doomed to drift from one high to the next. She was staying numb on drugs. She was also in and out of prison. She did not see her daughter much. Shelby was a breath of fresh air. Surely, a gift from God. I loved being with Rick on the truck, but it was not for me. I no longer had the Knotty Pine for employment. So I got a job at a sandwich factory. It was just a couple of blocks from our house. We made sandwiches for food trucks. I loved that job. Rick was gone on the truck most of the time. There was no one at home to go to. All I had waiting on me was an empty nest. So I got me a part-time job at a little bar around the corner. I needed to stay busy. So busy I was.

One day, Rick got home with a startling announcement. He said, "Start packing. We are moving to Oklahoma." I believe that would be the best thing for us. Lisa was out there, and hopefully, the other kids would follow. I needed a change. Bakersfield was nothing but a heartache to me. I would leave all the pain behind me. I needed a change—a new life, a fresh start. I would miss Colleen and Gina and Mom and Daddy. They were always there when I needed them. Mom and Daddy were not in the best of health. When would I get to see them again? I did not want to leave them. But I must go with my husband. I did know that the Greyhound bus would bring me home again if needed be. So here we go again. Oklahoma, here we come. I knew if Rick and I got out of Bakersfield, we could have a new start to let our love grow and see that this marriage works. Our friends helped us pack our belongings into a haul trailer. Boswell or bust. Once again, we were off to make a new start at the life we started together so many years ago—not a dime to our name. But we had a credit card that would get us there and on our feet. All we had right now was each other. This was the first time it had been this way. I felt like I had lived in a box long enough—time for wide-open spaces. I hoped we'd find again what we had lost. It had been eleven long, heartbreaking years since we sold that calf, pulled out of Boswell, Oklahoma, headed to Bakersfield for a short trip to try to regain custody of my boys. What a trip we went on. Once again, it was Boswell or bust, a new journey, a fresh start, back to where our love was young and new. This was another chance for our love to flourish. We left the pain of our shattered lives behind.

It took us three days, and here we were, sitting out on Mom and Dad's porch, planning our future. I really did not know anyone out here but Rick's family. It was lonely, but it was beautiful here. I loved to watch the lighting bugs that came out on hot summer nights—the lighting that lights up the sky at night during a storm. This was a peaceful place to unwind. Lisa and our little Brandon were going to move to Missouri. Her boyfriend got a good-paying job out there with Lisa's uncle. They would be joining him soon. There were not a lot of jobs in this area. I couldn't blame them for moving. We only got to spend a couple of weeks with Lisa and baby Brandon. When they finally left for Missouri to join Brandon's daddy, I missed Lisa and that baby boy so much. I could tell Rick missed them also.

Rick said, "Let's go to the lake and stay a month before we get a job."

It sounded good to me. So we got our camping gear together and headed for the lake. We set up our camp, made it real homey. We were all set up for a month at the lake—not worried about nothing but each other. The first few days were good. The July weather in Oklahoma was not the time to go to the lake for a month's vacation. It was so hot we could not breathe. The humidity soared. We are miserable. At night, when it cooled, the buzzing of the mosquitos began. So we packed up and went back to Mom and Dad's house. So much for a month at the lake.

Now it was time to go to get jobs. It was not hard to find jobs. I went to work at Franks café as a cook. Rick went to work at a sawmill. Now we needed our own place. When a place around here gets empty, someone is waiting to move in. Now Bryan and his girlfriend wanted to come out here and live with us. He said they were both drug addicts and wanted a new start. They wanted to live near us. He would not come without his girl. She was only seventeen at the time. As soon as she turned eighteen, we headed to Georgia to get them. He said, "Mom, we have $800 and can get our own place." That would have been nice. By the time we got there, he had no money and just kept telling us to lie after lie. Bryan's girlfriend Terry went to work with me at the café, and Bryan went to work with his dad at the sawmill. We finally found us a house of our own. I loved having Bryan nearby, but he brought a lot of drama into my life. He had a lot of problems. He drank way too much. I told the people at the store he was not old enough to drink. They still sold it to him anyway. He said he just couldn't forgive himself for what he did to us. I was beginning to believe it just an excuse for his degenerate lifestyle. We had told the kids many times it was not their fault. Things had changed. I no longer wanted the kids at home. I wanted them close to me but not under our roof. My love for my children would always be. I had a need for peace in my life. It took me years to admit, but peace was not what my boys gave me. I couldn't control their lives. I only had one thing to say about my life, and I said, "I have had enough sorrow for one lifetime."

I liked my job, and I worked hard to keep it. I felt at peace here in Oklahoma, the most beautiful place I have ever lived. There was no more looking over my shoulder. Then one day, all my fears came true when I got to work. One of the girls I worked with said, "I saw you on TV last night." My heart hit my stomach. I was not sure what she saw. I had feared this moment.

I asked, "What did you see?" She did say we were falsely accused of molesting our children and went to prison for life. I told her, "I cannot explain this in a couple of minutes, so we will talk when we have time." I thought to myself, *How can I explain this to someone else when I still do not know how that all happened?* All day I was in a tizzy. She never mentioned it again. It took a while before I sat down and talked to her about what had happened to us. I did try to explain it all to her. I felt good talking about it. I held it all inside me for so long. I was sure there were people around here that remembered when all this started. We lived in Boswell. I did not want to spend the rest of my life explaining this or trying to prove our innocence. I just wanted it all to go away and let us live our lives and try to find happiness. One day, I would wake up, and it would be behind me. After all these years, we still could use some counseling.

Sis called and said Mom was sick, and I needed to come. I went and stayed for a couple of weeks. I felt extremely uncomfortable in Bakersfield. I visited Mom, Colleen, and Gina. If anyone else wanted to see me, they came over to Colleen's house to visit with me. Mom got better for this time anyway. I was getting worse. No comfort in Bakersfield for me, not after living in beautiful and peaceful Oklahoma. I did not want to think about it, but Mom probably would not be around too much longer. She had suffered for so long with COPD, fighting for just one breath at a time. I was sure ready to get back to my life in Oklahoma. I missed Rick, and I had a job to get back to. Rick had gone back to driving a truck. I sure did not like to be alone. I worked a lot just to keep me busy. The holidays were the worst without my family. Now that Bryan and his girlfriend got their own place, I never saw him anymore. I guess he did not want me to see that he was drinking and doing drugs every day of his life. His little girlfriend worked her butt off to keep him supplied.

It was taking me time to adjust to Oklahoma. I was so used to being around my family. I had friends, but it was just not the same. I got a call from Johnnie. He said Tommie just got four years in prison. I did not even ask why. If they could just get out of Bakersfield, maybe they would do better. Carol had finally got out of Bakersfield. She had moved to Missouri with her sister. I would be glad when all my kids get out of Kern County. Everyone seemed to be just doing their own thing living their own lives. I probably should stop wishing we could all be together. Those boys chose to live a life of crime. I would never give up hope on my children. I would always pray they find peace one day.

New Year of 1997 came with a bang. Lisa's boyfriend had killed himself. He was just eighteen years old, leaving Lisa with a six-month-old baby. This was going to be hard on Lisa and Carol. They had each other and would make it through this. They had both went back to Bakersfield. Alvin's parents had his body flown back to Bakersfield for burial. Lisa came to visit for three weeks, and little Brandon had stolen his grandmas' heart. They headed back to Bakersfield. She said she would move back someday. I would hold her to it. Carol, Lisa, and Brandon all lived with Alvin's dad. Life had been rough on my girls. I knew they were safe at Al's. I just hated that they were in Kern County. I would keep praying for them all to find in life what makes them happy. The girls did have their mom with them.

I had made a manager at the café where I worked. This was a busy little café, and I loved my job. Rick was finally working in town. He was home every night. This was the way I like it. I hated being alone. My best friend Yvonne came out for her birthday. We threw her a party at the little bar down the road—the Tin Top. We lived in a small town, population of 280. There were more people on a city block in Bakersfield than there was in this whole town. I loved living in a small town. It reminded me of Coalinga, where I lived as a child.

On July 30, 1997. I turned forty-two today, and my dear mother died. I flew into Bakersfield to be with my siblings. Clovette could not make it. Mom did not want a funeral and did not want us kids to see her after she passed. I did not agree with this no funeral. This was for the loved ones to say goodbye. Her ashes were to be taken to Coalinga, California, and we scattered her ashes on her grandfather's grave. For now, Colleen wanted to keep her. I would make another trip out one day and follow up on Mom's wishes. Losing our parents was a part of life, and I knew Mom could finally breathe. I knew the pain would ease up with time. Colleen and Mom had always been close. It would be hard on her for a while, and she would live on. I felt bad that I did not live in Bakersfield. I knew Colleen needed me. Now she did not have Mom or me. She was a strong woman and would be fine. Wayne had always been a momma's boy. He also would be fine. Colleen was raising grandkids, two of the sweetest little girls. I believed they were three and four. I told her to move out here so I could help her with her babies. I knew she would not like it here—not enough was going on.

I was not so fond of my job anymore. My boss just did not show much appreciation. I worked hard for them. They would miss me if I go. I had put three years in here, and I went beyond my work details to see that I always did a good job. Now it was time to move on. I stayed home for a while, and that was not good for me. I needed to stay busy. There was a little bar called the Red Barn. It was in Durant, just 15 miles away. Rick would stop by there when he got off work. I met him down there one day and found myself a new job. I loved my new job and my new boss. Rick was out on the road again, so I worked as much as I could. We bought us a little place out in the country. The house was small and old, but it was ours, and we loved it out there. We got us some chickens to go on our little farm. Rick decided he wanted to be an over-the-road truck driver. So we sold our little house to our uncle. We planned to make money to buy us a bigger place in the country. He got a job where I could go with him. Off we went on a new chapter of our life.

Our first trip was out to California. This truck we were in just might not get us there. It finally broke down about three hours from

Bakersfield. When he called his boss, he cursed Rick out and told him he did not know how to drive a truck. Rick quit and called a friend in Bakersfield to come get us. So we stayed with Lisa till Rick made money to rent a car and went home where we belong. While I was in Bakersfield, Colleen would not speak to me. She got mad at me last year when I would not send her money. I knew she was all messed up on drugs. I was here, and she would not see me. She would not answer my calls, and this broke my heart. Colleen meant the world to me. She was my baby sister, and we had been through hell and back together. Johnnie was out right now, too busy to see his mom. He did come over to ask for a ride. I did not have a car, so he no longer needed me. Tomboy was in prison. Still I did not get to see him. It did not take Rick long to make money to head back to good old Oklahoma. We were off to one more new start.

Uncle said we could stay with him till we got our own place again. I went back to Red Barn, and Rick went back to driving a truck. We bought our own truck this time. When we had plenty of help at the Red Barn, I would go with Rick on the truck. One evening, coming in off the road with Rick, we stopped by the Red Barn. It was closed. I had keys, so I went in. Everything looked okay—just no one there. We went home, and there was a message on the phone. My boss was in the hospital, not doing well. I went to see her, and it was not good. She said, "Help my daughter run the Red Barn." I gave it my all, and it just did not work out at the Red Barn. My new boss spent the money as fast as I made it. I would come to work, and I would not have a beer to sell. She just did not know how to run a bar. So once again, it was time to move on. She did not last long, and one of the college girls was running the Red Barn, and it was too much for her. She asked me to help her. That worked for a short while. I bought her out, and now the Red Barn was mine. Rick was on the road a lot, so I just put myself into my work. I had a college crowd. They kept me busy. I loved it there. Rick would make it home for most weekends. That lasted a little over a year. The man that owned the building wounded to lease it to someone else. I had a blast there. The time went fast, and there was no time for sorrow. Life was getting better all the time. I left and went out to Bill Dog's

Saloon. That was another fast year. We worked hard and played even harder. Things went great there. I heard the Tin Top was for sale. I had just won $10,000 at the Indian casino. I explained to Bill Dog I had a chance to have my own place. He understood, and we moved on as friends. We met a lot of good people there, and we would be forever friends.

Rick had not been well. He had some real bad dizzy spells. We had been to doctors, and it seemed no one knew what was causing him to fall out and get dizzy. We had spent thousands of dollars for a doctor to tell him to change his pillow and take an aspirin. He had to give up this CDLs, no more driving a truck for him. We sold Rick's truck, and my winnings, we bought the Tin Top. It was now Tootie's Saloon—no more working for someone else. We stayed behind the bar in our trailer till we could find us a house. It did not take long to settle down in Bennington. We found a house to rent two blocks from the bar. It was a big old house. It had the biggest kitchen I had ever seen. This place was cold in the winter and hot in the summer. It was closed to work, so it would work for now. Our little bar was going well. Our house was way too close to our work. There were people at our door all the time, needing one thing or another. Bryan had a new girlfriend, and she had 2 acres in the country for sale. We bought it and moved out here to the country, and we love it. We had grandkids, kids, and chickens. Johnnie had finally settled down here. He gave me three wonderful grandkids and a beautiful daughter-in-law.

The years went so fast. I just did not know where it all went. I saw my children struggle with their lives. I had concluded I couldn't change what life had thrown at me. Over the years, I had learned not to take the way my boys turned out. Personally, I was not there to raise them. It was not my fault. Kern County took my chance to be a mother away from me. I did not have the power in me to fix what had been broken. I loved my children more than words could say. If only the district attorney and those who did this to us felt the guilt our poor children carry with them, maybe we could of together and help our children. No one would ever admit what they have done to our families. This would affect our families for generations to come.

When I sat down to write this book, I wrote the last chapter first. Much had happened since then, but I chose to include it all. I wrote this in October 2010. It had been twenty years since we walked free. I felt this was the appropriate time to share my story. Life interfered, and it took another decade for me to put this all into words. I would forever feel the pain of my past. I saw and felt the pain in my now-adult children's eyes and heard it in their voices. Even though my tears no longer fell every day, one or more of the children in these cases still cried every day. They were so young. They did not understand it. I was a grown woman, and I did not understand. I had finally excepted it. They may never accept it. After all these years, we were still trying to overcome what Kern County's justice system had done to us. This corrupted system tore up many families. Not only my children had these feelings. All the other children, as well as mine, couldn't find their way in life. They were all so full of anger, which made life so much harder than it should be. God bless our children. I still thank God every day for our freedom.

Rick and I had been able to do a few things, like going on a vacation, getting away from the rush of life, spending some needed time together, and seeing some beautiful places we had never seen before. Lisa took care of the bar, so we could go. First, we went to beautiful Colorado, where the mountains were high and the air was fresh—the most beautiful place I had ever seen. Once again, I felt tears running down my face. This time, they were happy tears. I had never seen so much beauty in my life. I squeezed Rick's hand and smiled through my tears. The Teton mountains were just breathtaking. Rick and I were the perfect age to enjoy each other. We had been at Tooties for nine years now. The time just flew by. We had a good time here. Our little Lisa took incredibly good care of our bar. That made it easier for us. Rick always asked, "Where does your book end?" There were so many more and so many people to tell their stories.

I made a trip to Bakersfield to see my little sister. I decided to talk to the people that were in our case. Here are their stories they would like for me to share. First, I asked my baby sister Colleen what she would like me to write in my book. She said, "Put it simple." All she wanted me to add was she lost both of her daughters because of all this, our baby Amanda to death. She was murdered and left in a motel room in Bakersfield. A drug deal went wrong—and Windy to drugs. She was in and out of prison, just like my boys. Colleen never settled down for too long at a time. Then her health went bad. When she lost her daughters, she never got out of bed again. After five or six years in bed, sis asked me to please take her life support off. I loved her enough to set her free. She died on July 1, 2016. RIP, sissy. I love you more.

Next, I asked Wayne Forsyth and his wife Stephanie to come over and talk to me. I was so sorry that I waited for twenty years. They were both genuinely nice people. I had only met Wayne F. a couple of times before trial. I met Stephanie when we were in the county jail. We all shared a cell, C-44. At first, Wayne said he really did not want to talk about the past. Then once we got to talk, he said it felt rather good talking to someone that understood his story. He said when he first heard about all this, he was at Stephanie's house, and he had seen it in the newspaper. He told Stephanie, "I know those people, and I know that is not true." Colleen and Wayne had been married but had since separated and went their own way. He said he thought to himself he should go see Colleen and see if there was anything he could do to help. Once he got up there, Colleen told him he would probably get arrested also. He should go see her lawyer. Her lawyer told him they were fixing to arrest him. Wayne said, "It scared me, but I was not that worried because I knew that this had never happened." He said he was running scared, hiding out over at his girlfriend's house. He could not figure out why we were all still in jail. Steph said they had been around looking for Wayne. They told her they would get her harboring Wayne. They threatened her with her own children.

They finally caught up with them both, charging Wayne with not only our case but another case as well with Steph's children and some kids in their neighborhood. They thought it would end before it got started—wrong. The day they were convicted, they took Wayne into another courtroom and wanted him to make a plea on this new case. He said, "You just sentenced me to 280 years for something that never happened. Take me to trial." The court told them they could all just go to prison with the Pitts if they did not take their deal. They all knew we were all innocent, so the rest of them took a deal. Wayne sat in county jail almost a year before they dropped charges on him. The rest of those innocent people had to live their lives signed up as a sex offender. After Wayne got out, he and Steph had a rough time. They let drugs numb them from all their pain. After hitting bottom, they both found the Lord, and he has saved their lives. Amen. They were blessed with their children and grandchildren, hoping to maybe leave Bakersfield behind them someday. I love you both.

Another story that had never been told. I talked with Carla. She was never officially charged in our case. She wanted to share her story with the world so they would know what our justice system could do. They put her through hell. In the very beginning, when we were first arrested, the officials did not know the difference between Carla and Gina. When they arrested Gina, Carla's name was on Gina's warrant. That is how well they knew us. They did not. Carla said she knew she would be arrested. She was Colleen and Gina's best friend. She just tried moving on with her life. She found a new love and was trying to be happy. She said she was living in fear, knowing this never happened, and her best friends were in jail. She kept waiting for them to let us go, knowing this never happened. She said at times, she felt she would go crazy thinking about all this.

Then came December. Christmas was near. She was decorating her tree, trying to bring the holiday cheer. There was a knock at her door. When she opened the door, two Kern County sheriffs stood in her doorway. She knew what they wanted. They told her they were taking her in for questioning. When they got to the county jail, they placed her in a small room. Carla had lost her kids about a year ago. They told her they knew she had been molesting her four-year-old son. They had counts they could charge her with. They said, "Tell me about the Pitts case." She told them she knew the things they were saying about the Pitts are not true. When they knew she was not on their side, they left the room. She was crying uncontrollably. They knew she was scared to death. She found a recorder under the table. When they came back into the room, she told them that yes, she did want to testify for her family.

They said, "Let's go." She thought they were taking her home. She kept asking, "Where are we going?" and they would not answer. I could tell by the tears in her eyes and the trembling in her body as she told me what they had done to her. Her fears were real. I believed every word she told me. Carla said, "After about two hours, we pulled up to a jail in a little town called Independence, California. They booked me in as Jane Doe. I felt as if my life was being threatened. I lay there for three or four days, chained to the bed."

She continued, "I am not going to lay here and just let them kill me. I screamed and screamed and screamed till they took me to the hospital in Bishop. I told the doctor there what has been happening to me. I told him everything all about my family. He acted as if he believed me. They gave me a shot of something, and it calmed me down. I was very sedated. When I returned to the jail, there were two deputy district attorneys waiting on me. They told me I would testify in the Pitts case. They handed me a piece of paper that told me what I needed to say. They really thought they had scared me into testifying for them. I told them they were crazy, and I knew like this had never ever happened. Once they had seen I was not doing it, they got up and left." The jailor just let her go in a pair of shorts and a tank top. It was after midnight, dark and cold. She made a call to her boyfriend and made it home. They never called again about the Pitts case. She said, "This is when I found my new best friend, Mr. Meth." She wanted to be numb. She could not believe that my friends that had been her family since she was twelve years old were locked up for something. She knew they did not do it, but she couldn't help them. She was forced to live my life without them. After we got out, I had run into Carla from time to time. All these years doing drugs really took a toll on our dear friend. RIP, Carla. You left us too soon. I love you like a sister.

Cliff and Clovette Pitts—their six years on the run was extremely hard on them. They ran from state to state, living in the mountains, living off the land with the fear of being caught and losing their children to the evil hands of Kern County. They finally settled down in Georgia with an older man that needed a family. They, for sure, needed a friend. They taught the kids what they could so they would not get too behind in the schooling. Cliff would work when he could, always with the fear of someone recognize him and report him to the law. The years on the run tore through their love. When this was all over, they went their separate ways. Cliff lived nearby with his new wife. He had always been a hardworking man. Clover and her kids and grandkids and a couple of great-great-grandkids moved to Alabama. Because of Clovette's health and choices, she made her life way too short. Sis, you are the wind beneath my wings. Clovette passed away on April 19, 2018. I love and miss you, Clover Dill. RIP. On April 29, 2020, we lost Cliff to COPD. Love and miss you, brother. We will meet again.

My brother Wayne Dill was the only brother that had to put up with the four of us girl. He was our baby, and we had him spoilt rotten. He never figured out what he wanted in life. At the age of forty-seven, Wayne passed away from cancer. His son Billy Dill and his beautiful wife Nicole lived near me. They added a lot of cheer and happiness to my life, three girls and one boy. I love watching them grow up. I feel blessed to have them in my life. RIP, my little brother. Love and miss you always.

Our dear friend Gina still lived in Bakersfield. She has raised her children and now helps with her grandchildren. I always stop by when I make it to Bakersfield to give my dear friend a hug. Moe May, I wish you happiness forever. I love you, my dear friend.

My children—I could write a whole entire book on the lives of my children. After Kern County got a hold of them, they had a hard time coping with everyday life. There were good stories of the time. They were all happy, and there was a time when no happiness to be found. Now I saw the mistakes I had made with my children, thinking that my love for them would heal everything. Wrong, I would go on loving my children, and most of my children would go on not trusting anyone—having a hard time pushing through the years of their lives. Carol, our oldest daughter, lived here near us. We did not see much of her. She stayed to herself most of the time. She said to me once, "I will always be that eleven-year-old little girl they took from you guys so many years ago." She was still not trusting a soul—never married or had children.

Johnnie, next by age, left about six years ago. He called about three years ago and said, "I am doing my own thing." His ex-wife and my grandchildren lived close to us. I had stopped crying over Johnnie, but I would never stop loving him or praying for him to come home. I love and miss you, John boy. He had given us five grandkids, three great-grandkids, and a beautiful daughter-in-law Dana. Tommie had been in and out of prison, more in than out, till he finally found the love of his life. I believed Debra changed Tommie. He did not have to stay drugged up to be numb. She taught him to love, and now he was no longer alone. She would follow him anywhere. The two of them joined the carnival and traveled for a couple of years. He worked hard to provide for his beautiful wife. About eight years after they married, Debra got sick. She died a painful death with cancer. Tommie went back to his old ways. Now he is forty-five years old, here at home with Mom and Dad. He is not well. He has heart disease. Finally, after all these years, he slowed down enough to make it home.

Then we have our little Lisa. She has given us two wonderful grandsons. In my eyes, of all our children, she has been the happiest, still full of life. She loves and takes care of all of us, old folk. Bryan also lives near us. He has one son that lives in Georgia. Bryan still drinks way too much. He is a functioning alcoholic. He is a hard worker most of the time. He just cannot find happiness and has a life full of drama. Most of the grandkids are turning teenagers. They do not need Grandma and Grandpa anymore. They have their friends. Still at the end of every day, I pray for God to bless our children.

Rick, my wonderful husband, the love of my life—here we are thirty-seven lone years later, growing old together just like we planned so many years ago. We have a little farm, lots of chickens, and the right time of the year, Rick has the most beautiful gardens full of vegetables that you have seen. I have my family dinner. Sometimes, they all show up, and sometimes, it is just a few of us. Rick and I both have lost both our moms and dads. Our kids and grandkids are busy with their lives. We have our bar up for sale. When it's sold, we want to do some traveling again. I want to see something that takes my breath away. I want to smell some flowers, the ones I have no name for, the ones that I have seen all my life and never took the time to embrace their beauty—maybe go fishing where we have never fished before.

Rick is now sixty-eight, and I would say he is in good health, and I am spritely sixty-four and ready to go. Despite all Rick and I have been thought, no matter how many stumbling blocks, we have made it over. We have good times and bad times. Now there should be plenty of time to make many more great memories. We are trying to put the past behind us, trying to balance the past pain and the future smiles that lay ahead of us. One thing I know, no matter where we go or what we do, I know Rick will always be there to wipe these mother's tears from my eyes while I cry for my children—my babies that I loved and lost in 1985 to Kern County and their injustice. When I dream of all that could have been, I remember then what they did to us—the one thing I can never put behind me. The one big question I will always seek, the one I will never know the answer too—I will always wonder how life could have been.

Marcella Pitts, AKA Tootie

It took me over thirty years to write this book. In 2017, my house burnt down, and my book went up in smoke, along with everything I owned. A friend of mine had most of my notes. When the shock of the fire was over and we settled into our new place, I restarted my book. I could write for years. Most days came with a new story to tell. The lives of our children carried the scars of 1985 with them every day. There was nothing I could ever say or do to help them with what they have been through. Once our trial was over, they were no longer needed. They did not even have each other. They were all alone to face their fears. When we all came home, they all thought Mom was here now. She could fix it. I also believed I could. Believe me, I gave it my all. Our love for each other would conquer everything. All we needed was to be together. I never even thought of helping myself. I had just been to hell and back. This had changed us all. I was so in love with the children they took from me. When we got home, they were no longer babies. They were young adults. We never took the time to get help with what we had been through. I had been home, and all coming together was supposed to fix it all. It had taken many years for me to find peace again. Some of my children did not like themselves and did not trust anyone. They had never found peace. Yes, I know my children loved me, and I also knew the seven years without their mom and dad changed them. The only one that loved them was locked up like an animal, not able to get to them.

Now that we are getting older, we enjoy life a little more. The kids come home from time to time. We have not all been together in years. I still pray every night for the Lord to bring my babies home to me.

I hope you have enjoyed reading my book. It has taken me love, sweat, tears, and lots of years to finally say I am finished. If you were one of the ones that also lived this nightmare, I hope something I have written in the words of my book brings you a moment of peace.

About the Author

I have learned in life that it's not what is dealt to you. It's how you deal with what is dealt to you. This is the first time I have written and published a book. When the documentary *The Witch Hunt* came out, it gave me the incentive to finish writing my book. I wanted to share with the world that there are innocent people in prison. I was sentenced to 373 years in prison for a crime that I never committed. My children's life was like mine, and my family went to shambles. I was married to the man of my dreams. Our lives were torn up by the injustice of this world. We were separated for almost seven long years. We were so in love with our children, but they took them from us. We came home to rebellious teenagers. They had no trust for anyone. I believed our love for each other would hold us together. Love was just not enough to fix what had been broken in each of us. We spent our lives trying to get back what had been taken from us.

I hope the words of my book would show how a family has spent our whole lives fighting to get back what was taken from each of us. Here is the story of *A Mother's Tears*, a mother trying to get her family back, trying to hold things together.

Thank you, Kristal Farley, for helping me put my book together. Thank you, my BFFs Rick, Yvonne, Pam, and Misty, for holding me together.

God bless.

CPSIA information can be obtained
at www.ICGtesting.com
Printed in the USA
LVHW030508200821
695646LV00001B/227

9 781662 424953